Error-Proofing Your Research

I0643703

ERROR-PROOFING YOUR RESEARCH

COMMON MISTAKES AND HOW TO ADDRESS THEM

JOSE EOS TRINIDAD

BlueBooks

BlueBooks

an imprint of
ATENEO DE MANILA UNIVERSITY PRESS
Bellarmine Hall, Katipunan Avenue
Loyola Heights, Quezon City
P.O. Box 154, 1099 Manila, Philippines
Tel. (632) 426-59-84 / Fax (632) 426-59-09
E-mail: unipress@ateneo.edu
Website: www.ateneopress.org

Copyright 2019 by Ateneo de Manila University and Jose Eos Trinidad

Cover design by Mikaela Montano
Book design by Cielo Castro

All rights reserved. No part of this publication may be reproduced, stored in a retrieval system, or transmitted in any form or by any means, electronic, mechanical, photocopying, recording, or otherwise, without the written permission of the Publisher.

The National Library of the Philippines CIP Data
Recommended entry:

Trinidad, Jose E.
Error-proofing your research : common mistakes and how to address them / Jose Eos Trinidad. – Quezon City : ATENEO DE MANILA UNIVERSITY PRESS, [2019], c2019.
pages ; cm

ISBN 978-971-550-908-4

1. Report writing – Study and teaching (Higher) 2. Education, Higher – Research. I. Title.

371.302810711 LB1047.3 P920190032

CONTENTS

INTRODUCTION

In high school, students are required to do research as proof of their academic ability or intellectual grasp of a subject. In college, the same students will be asked to write their undergraduate thesis, which will again have them do some formal research using citations, professional language, and clear arguments. As these students pass from college to their first job, they will still have to do some type of research—probably not with the same formality as in school, but it is research nonetheless. Those in a corporate job will have to do some market research; those who become teachers will have to learn what pedagogical methods work for their classes; those who become entrepreneurs will need to research about their company and their competitors. Of course, those who become scientists will have to publish research; artists will have to research their work, subject, or craft; doctors will have to keep abreast of new medications and treatments; and inventors will have to create new technologies.

More and more, we live in an interconnected **knowledge economy**. Most of the people who advance in this type of economy are those who are able to effectively use their critical thinking and intellectual skills. Advancing in society is no longer about mere physical hard work or personal connections. Social and economic advancement involves being learned, entering professions, introducing innovations, having the ability to communicate ideas, having leadership skills, and using one's creativity and intellectual gifts for the good of oneself and society. Inasmuch as hard work and perseverance are important, we must also acknowledge how contemporary society privileges these intellectual, collaborative, and thinking skills.

Clearly, learning the principles and basics of research helps people practice the skills necessary for participation in a knowledge economy. When you learn research, you learn how to distinguish correct and accurate information from false ones; how to think through competing options and alternatives; how to clarify your reasoning, thoughts, and arguments; how to understand different people's positions and ideas; and how to work independently with discipline and integrity. Learning research is not just about writing up a research paper; it is about using the research process to learn important skills of critical thinking, problem solving, decision-making, effective communication, and personal organization.

Some students think that doing research is an impractical exercise because they are not thinking of a research job in the future. However, the skills you learn from the research process are applicable in whatever field you end up pursuing. Businessmen must know how to weigh different options; teachers must know how to solve dilemmas that arise in their classrooms; politicians and policy makers must know how to make decisions that are beneficial to most people; doctors must practice effective communication with their patients; and rank-and-file workers will benefit from knowing how to organize their resources and manage their time. When viewed in this way, researching is actually a very **practical exercise** that provides opportunities for students to learn important life skills.

Now, most research books will inform you what to do and how to act. They will tell you how to think about a research problem, how to create surveys, how to write about your findings, and how to interpret your results. This book, however, is a little different. This book tells you more about what not to do—that is, the **research mistakes** you can avoid.

But why read a book about mistakes? First, learning about mistakes prior to writing the research helps you recognize what practices to avoid. In medicine, they say that **prevention is better than cure**. In the same way with research, knowing what to avoid is possibly more efficient than changing your research once the mistake has already been committed. Some research mistakes can be quite costly in terms of time (e.g. wrong structure for research), effort (e.g. wrong data collection instrument), or reputation (e.g. plagiarism or falsification of data). By knowing what to be careful with, you can actually concentrate on telling your reader about your main argument. By avoiding common pitfalls, you are concentrating your energies on the more important facets of your research. By knowing these mistakes, you can prepare how to respond when they happen.

Second, **learning what not to do** is sometimes **more powerful** than being told what to do. Through my teaching research courses in the university, I have realized that students learn better when they know what not to do, in addition to knowing what to do. Sometimes, the lesson can be self-evident—even inescapably obvious—but people still do not heed it. Thus, it is interesting that greater learning can actually happen when mistakes are pointed out. By clarifying what are not admissible or permitted, students will not have an excuse about being ignorant of the expectations for research. After all, most research mistakes happen not because people consciously want to break rules but because they are ignorant that they have made a mistake or broken a rule. By reading all of these mistakes in this book, they are less likely to say that they are ignorant of what they should not be doing.

Third, understanding research mistakes serves as a **complement** to the proper conduct of the research process. One must not think that this book is the only book you will need when doing research; rather, this is a complementary material to what you learn from a typical research book. It is not a substitute but a means for deepening insight into the research process. As a complementary material, it seeks to show subtle and explicit ways when research can be done wrongly or inaccurately. By showing these mistakes and solutions, the book reinforces the lessons in typical research books.

Of course, some may argue that a book focusing on research mistakes robs students of the experience of learning by trial and error. Some may even argue that the book has too narrow a focus that it prevents students from being creative and critical. On the contrary, I believe the book provides helpful tips so that researchers can focus on the content of the research rather than the avoidable mistakes on the structure or writing of the research. It will be a better use of time if teachers point out the substantial mistakes in the content or logic rather than the mistakes of wrong citations or incorrect tables. The book provides students, teachers, and researchers with the minimum expectations for a good research so that they can focus more on the content and argumentation.

With these ideas in mind, the book hopes to help students, teachers, and other researchers identify research mistakes and learn how to address them—either by preventing them or by fixing them when they happen. For students, this book could help reduce the difficulty of writing research by showing what are common pitfalls and what are the expectations for good research. For teachers, the book helps in identifying common mistakes that students can commit. Teachers can use these identified mistakes either when teaching students about the research process or when pointing out to students what their mistakes are. For researchers, the book can be a helpful refresher for subtle mistakes that can crop up every now and then with research projects. Whether you are a beginner in research or a teacher of it, I hope the book provides you with a comprehensive guide to addressing research mistakes.

The six chapters of the book follow the usual progression of a research and within the chapters are sections that talk about specific mistakes that can be addressed, avoided, or fixed. Chapter 1 talks about mistakes in the **research process**, particularly those that relate to the research's feasibility and researcher's personal attitude toward research. It shows how mistakes can happen even before you start thinking about the research question. Chapter 2 focuses on **conceptualization** mistakes that come as you think about the research question and argument. It also talks about how research can be wrongly conceived because of mistakes when doing the literature review.

Chapter 3 highlights mistakes that happen with **research methods** and **instruments**, especially with obtaining qualitative and quantitative data. Aside from mistakes in collecting data, the chapter also introduces mistakes with unethical conduct in doing research. Chapter 4 is about mistakes in the **analysis** and **presentation** of your research, particularly those on improper tables and figures in quantitative research and on wrong use of quotes in qualitative research. In addition, the chapter also talks about how data can sometimes be inaccurately interpreted or discussed.

Chapter 5 emphasizes the mistakes that arise when **writing** the research. These mistakes include those that happen with the research structure, paragraphs, sentences, words, and even punctuation. Aside from discussing mistakes in grammar and usage, the chapter also talks about mistakes when doing citations—whether footnote or in-text citations. The final chapter shows common mistakes that arise as you prepare to submit your research for **publication**. Since not many people are familiar with the publication process, the book adds this section to inform readers about common challenges when submitting the research to a journal.

The research mistakes in the book do not concentrate on any singular discipline but are often shared among different research papers in different fields. Of course, certain mistakes are unique to particular disciplines, but this book hopes to be more general in identifying the common pitfalls that you can avoid or fix. You can read the whole book chronologically, or you can concentrate on a chapter at a time to know what to avoid. You can refer your students to particular sections if you are pointing out their mistakes, or you can discuss the section before or after students submit their research. You may even want to just skim the contents and focus on certain ideas.

Showing these mistakes is not about making your research free from errors because there will likely be other errors not included in this book. But by identifying these mistakes, you can be more discerning and deliberate about what you write, and thus have fewer mistakes in your research paper. By reducing your mistakes, your reader—whether it be your teacher, professor, reviewer, or just your general reader—can focus on your arguments and not on the mistakes committed.

CHAPTER 1
MISTAKES IN THE RESEARCH PROCESS

Before even conceptualizing the research project, there are already a few mistakes that people often make, and these mistakes can be very costly in terms of time and effort. In this chapter, I talk about the first few mistakes committed by people who are beginning to work on a research project. The chapter talks about lapses in understanding the purpose of research, making smart use of time, or assessing the feasibility of a particular project. As I outline these mistakes, I also talk about ways to address them. By knowing these mistakes in advance and doing preemptive techniques, you will save yourself the time and effort that these mistakes can cost.

1.1 Unclear purpose and audience

When doing a research project on your own, it can sometimes seem that you are merely writing for yourself or documenting ideas so that you can have something to refer to. Even when you do research with others, there could be this assumption that one only writes for the group. Thus, I emphasize that one of the first mistakes people make is to assume that they only write the **research for themselves**. Sometimes, the research is not even written for oneself; it is just simply written out of compliance.

If you are in senior high school or college, you will probably be asked to write a research paper. If you are currently working, you would likely have taken a course on research. If you are researching in your job, you might have made this mistake of not knowing who you are writing for. If you are teaching research, you will likely have seen students' papers not clear about their purpose and audience.

So what does it mean to do research with an unclear purpose or audience?

Unclear purpose means that the author does not know what the research is for—the ultimate end of the research. Of course, one knows when one is writing to fulfill a school requirement: a term paper, a thesis, or a dissertation. One knows when one is writing to publish in a peer-reviewed journal. Despite this knowledge, it is worth noting that not all research projects are the same, and there are **salient differences** in types. Some research is used for policy decisions, and so will need to be brief and to the point. Some research is used for marketing products, so a discussion of the product is necessary. Some are done to obtain practical solutions to real-world problems while others are intended to extend our conceptual understanding of natural and social phenomena. Some are rigid in the structure of the final output while some are more organic and free-form. From these examples, we see how different research projects have different aims or purposes.

A second mistake related to this first one is about **unclear audience**, which means that the author does not have the reader in mind when writing the research. If one is clear about the aims or purposes of the research, it is easier to clarify it for one's audience. However, knowing the purpose does not immediately translate to knowing one's audience. One's readers can include policy professionals, businesspeople, literary writers, art critics, sociologists, economists, academics, students, or lay people. Within each of these groups, the readers will come with their own prior knowledge and understanding of your topic or research question.

Since not all research projects are the same, it is important to clarify from the start **what your research is about** and **who it is for**. There are a few practical things to keep in mind when addressing this mistake: At different points in your research, try to refresh (or keep on clarifying for yourself) the main motivation for writing the research. Knowing your motivation will help you think more thoroughly about where to spend your time on and what to write about. Given your limited time and resources, clarifying the purpose of your study can help focus your research. Two questions that you may want to ask yourself when making decisions for your research are: *How does this help the research's purpose?* and *What value is added to the research?*

Another helpful practice is clarifying the final output and the audience for that final output. If you are writing a thesis or term paper, think about the people who will be reading your paper. Even if you are not yet sure who your panelists will be, it will be good to have specific people in the back of your mind—and consciously ask yourself what they will look for in your research. If you are writing for a peer-reviewed journal, search for the specific journal you want to write for. By doing this, you will know the writing conventions, expectations, and aims of this journal. Even if in the end you are not published in that journal, it will still be helpful to orient and focus how you write.

Lastly, no matter who it is you are writing for, **specific sections** of your research should be **accessible to a wider audience**. Your introduction, discussion, and conclusion sections must be comprehensible to someone who will ask you in a restaurant or a family event what your research is about. This is not a suggestion to water down your research but is an invitation to let a wider audience understand your main research arguments. Your methods and results sections may use a specialized vocabulary in your discipline or subdiscipline, and it will be best to write in a way that acknowledges your audience's prior knowledge. For example, if you are writing for social psychologists, you will have to clarify what they already know and state how your research adds to what they already know.

When you are starting a research project, one of the crucial first tasks is to clarify your research purpose and audience. Knowing this will help you save a lot of time and give you enough criteria to make informed decisions about what to include in your research.

1.2 Procrastination

From teaching research classes, I know that variations of the scenario below are almost always going to happen:

> A group paper was assigned at the beginning of the semester. During the semester, the students read some things here and there, but did not write down anything because they believed that they needed to read up more or because they had other more pressing things to attend to (possibly from other classes). During the weekend or night before it was due, the students were furiously typing on their Google Document, all while Facebook messaging one groupmate who was clearly "ghosting" them. One member noticed that this groupmate had *seen-zoned* them and threatened to remove that delinquent member from their group. This member did some work—measly and sloppy. When the day of the submission came, they printed the paper just half an hour before handing it in; it was literally hot off the printer! When the teacher began checking, there were so many grammatical and spelling mistakes that she was unable to concentrate on the main ideas. The group got an F, and one member incurred everyone else's ire.

Of course, the scenario above is an exaggeration but it does tell us a whole lot about how **cramming** can be unhelpful for writing. Before talking about how one can address this issue of time management, it will be good to ask: *why do people procrastinate?*

On the one hand, there will always be many other things that will be more urgent than one's research: an organization's project, a family concern, a test in another subject, or a social media post that must be responded to. There is actually research to suggest that procrastination happens because of people's desire for **immediate gratification**.[1] This is why people try to put things off until later when it could be done now. Because writing may take time and the rewards (if there are any) are not as fast and apparent, people desire to use their time in activities that give greater immediate rewards. On the other hand, these sorts of research will have to be juxtaposed with other research that suggests that there is wisdom to academic cramming, which helps foster creativity and flow.[2] Whatever is your perspective on procrastination, there are some clear disadvantages if such practice prevents you from doing a good job in your research.

One way to avoid procrastination is through **time management**. Specifically, the time management technique should "reduce anxiety and fear and emphasize the satisfaction and rewards of completing tasks."[3] Having techniques that heighten anxiety, emphasize large tasks, and increase stress may actually be counter-productive. To manage one's time, it will be good to have a flexible outline of things to do that does not have to be a minute-by-minute list of all tasks at hand. Time management may also be carried out by **chunking tasks** so that the result is not one big output at the end of the term but smaller (and more manageable) tasks that can be completed weekly. You will know best how to manage your time and there are many resources for time management; this section just emphasizes the need for you to be aware of how you plan to manage your time.[4] Although there is no set rule on how much time to devote to your research, here are suggested chunks and time allotment:

- Pre-reading and generating ideas for a research question (2 – 3 weeks)
- Designing research, data collection, and analysis (3 – 4 weeks; this may include the research ethics application)
- Organizing and writing introduction and literature review sections (3 – 4 weeks; you can do this while waiting for the research ethics application to be approved)
- Data collection for interviews or surveys (2 – 4 weeks but it may take longer if your participants need more time to prepare for interviews. Remember that you will need to transcribe the answers during this time, too.)
- Analysis and writing the results section (2 – 3 weeks, depending on how detailed you want your results to be)
- Interpretation and writing the discussion section (2 weeks)
- Editing the research prose and citations (2 weeks)

Again, these steps only provide a quick snapshot of how much time research might take. If you devote yourself to the research, you may be able to write it much more quickly than the time suggested above. If your research entails more data collection or deeper engagements (or if you have other priorities), it will definitely take much longer to finish.

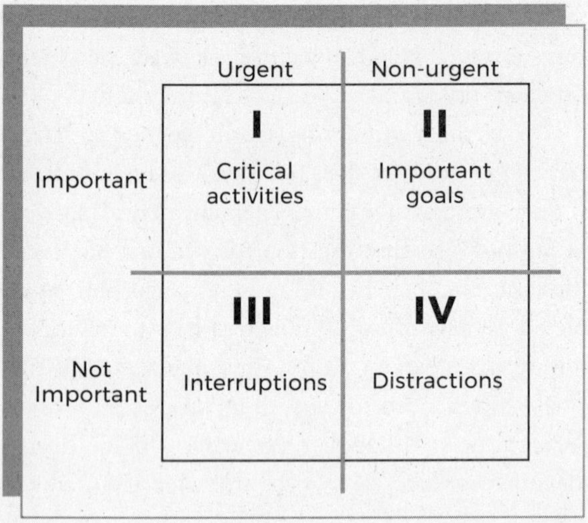

Figure 1. Eisenhower's Urgent-Important Matrix from Dimick (2015)

Another way of addressing procrastination is by knowing your **motivation** for doing work, particularly with how you think and the way you talk to yourself. When working on your research, what are the "scripts" that run in your mind? Do you think of your research as just something that needs to be over and done with or do you believe that your research will have some use, whether for you or for other people? Procrastination is oftentimes as much about motivation as it is about time management and organization. For example, one can say that "I don't have enough time and so I'll delay this research until I'm freer." But this script can be changed to "I only have 30 minutes right now. What can I write or accomplish within this 30-minute window?" This change in script needs to be a deliberate act for the one writing since the tendency is to use the automatic script of not having enough time. [5]

Lastly, since there will always be many things that will eat up your time, it will help to consider US President Dwight Eisenhower's **urgent/important matrix** (see Figure 1). In it, you see that there are particular decisions or actions deemed important and urgent, important but not urgent, not important but urgent, and not important and not urgent. For each of the boxes, there are corresponding ways of addressing them.[6] There is a hierarchy of doing important and urgent things first and doing those that are not important and not urgent last (if they should be done at all). I am not assuming that research will always be in your urgent and important quadrant, but depending on your life situation, you will have to clarify the position of research in your hierarchy of things to do. For some people, like researchers and graduating students, this will be at the top while for some who are doing this as a minor requirement, it might just be an added "inconvenience." Realistically assessing the importance and urgency of your research will help you decide how much time to devote to it. Be careful, though, of the tendency to put important things last because of how difficult they seem.

1.3 Neglecting guidelines, rubrics, and instructions

One sure way of wasting time is by neglecting the instructions that are offered in journal websites or thesis requirement syllabi. If you find yourself falling into this, you will realize that this wastes not only your time but also that of your co-authors or adviser. Inability to **follow instructions** at the start can lead you to change the citation format midway, or when you have already done all your research, to re-write whole sections because your paper's organization is not the preferred mode for the journal or the thesis. If you are working with an adviser, these mistakes in following guidelines will make your adviser focus on these small lapses rather than on the content of your research. If you research is peppered with these mistakes, your adviser might just give up and say that you have to rewrite everything following the guidelines that were given.

When writing for a **journal**, you should visit its website and view two important links. First, it is best to click on the journal's "Aims and scope" to see the types of articles the journal publishes. This connects with the earlier point about knowing the purpose and audience of your research. Some things to note is if the journals publish empirical and conceptual studies, if they are limited to particular geographic issues or topics, if there are methods they prefer, and so on. If you feel that your research matches the journal's aim, the second thing you should look at is the journal's "Instruction for authors" since this will tell you the practical things the journal is looking for. These include word limit, spelling preference (whether British or American English), citation style, paper structure, ethics approval, and peer review process. Knowing these things will help you plan for your writing, particularly if the journal is strict on the word count and citation style.

When writing for your **thesis** or **dissertation**, you should see your department or school's guidelines for your research. It is best to clarify the citation style since making these changes will be difficult when you are already done with your entire research. The social and natural sciences usually prefer the American Psychological Association's in-text citations, while fields in the humanities, history, and business prefer the Chicago Manual of Style's footnote citations. It is also important to clarify the expectations in terms of the average length of a thesis, paper size, margins, front matter and back matter, spacing, font, format for headings, and so on. Although some professors or research advisers will not care about the format, there will be those who might concentrate on your formatting mistakes rather than see the value of what is written in your research.

Aside from journals, theses, and dissertations, certain conferences have their particular **presentation** formats as well. Thus, if you are working on a presentation for a conference, it is best to know how long your presentation will be and how much time is devoted to other people's questions. Schools also have template slides for professors and students to use when presenting in conference; it is best to know if your school has these templated slides. Poster presentations are also avenues for your research to be presented, and it will be good to know the dimensions and the necessary ideas needed in your poster.

Some may argue that this is such a small thing to fuss about but there will be people who will make a big deal out of these small mistakes. When working on research, the amount of scrutiny, discipline, and meticulousness should be present in both the investigative part and the writing part. To be thorough in following instructions and guidelines is a mark of one's commitment to the work of research, and in practical terms, can actually save someone—and those around that person—a lot of time.

1.4 Infeasibility of research project

Sometimes a beginning researcher or student can think of a truly interesting research project and write a commendable research proposal, but this does not necessarily lead to the **execution** of the project. An example is a student who had a good research question comparing traditional and non-traditional schools, and even wrote a very promising proposal that had an extensive literature review. After writing the proposal, he went on to write an equally promising research ethics application with different consent forms, interview guides, and detailed processes. However, when he was about to go to the schools and ask for the teachers to be interviewed, he was politely informed that the school was not open to being researched on. Another example is a researcher who wanted to write about traffic in Metro Manila but did not have the data to back up her claims. She knew theoretically what should be done but she did not have empirical evidence to support her arguments.

The lesson from the two cases is clear: Before undertaking any research project, proposal, or even question, you must first ask if it is indeed **feasible** to do this type of research. As can be discerned from the cases, you have to know if the research respondents or institution will be open to your research project. It will be a good idea to ask the proprietors, administrators, or village officials if they are open to supporting your research. Without their support, even the best research projects will have a difficult time to get off the ground. This lesson might seem like a no-brainer but you will be surprised at how many students and researchers write their proposals without getting any permission from the people who will need to say yes to the research being done in their premises.

Another thing to make sure is that you complete your research within the **time allotted** for it. If you are a graduating senior, you will have around one year to work on your research. But this is quite imprecise since you will need to leave time for your readers or panelists to read your paper, some more time for you to make revisions, and a little more time for editing, formatting, printing, binding and so on. One of the key issues with research feasibility is to make sure you have enough time to gather your data: Will your interviewers be available within your timeline? Will you be able to get enough survey respondents? Will your research ethics clearance be done soon? You will have to see how you can compress and organize your time so that your research will be completed in the amount of time you have foreseen.

Another key to ensuring the feasibility of a research is by doing a **pilot study** prior to rolling out a full study. Pilot studies are either *trial runs* that are small-scale versions of the entire study or *test runs* that assure the viability of a particular research instrument (e.g. surveys, interview guides, etc.).[7] Doing a pilot study with a small sample helps you see the gaps in your research, other questions to ask respondents, how best to roll out a study, or emergent themes you can focus on.

Having a *pilot research survey* can give you insights into what questions were vague or which items were difficult to answer. It can also give you insights into potential practical problems that can arise like the unavailability of internet access or the inability of some respondents to follow instructions. Having *pilot interviews* can help you see what people's usual views are, how they react to particular questions, or what are practical ways for respondents to feel comfortable. Additionally, pilot interviews can help you in crafting questions for your surveys so that it will be easier for you to group ideas or categories. For example, if your pilot interviews yield categories about students' study habits, you can have these options already written in the survey instrument.

When starting a research project, you must make sure that it is feasible. Among the things you need to make sure are getting *approval* for research to be done with a certain population, taking into account the *time allocation* for your research, and doing *pilot studies* to ascertain that you will get the data needed for your research.

1.5 Group conflicts

One of the things that surprised me when I started teaching research is that the most common problems are not about citations, concepts, or research structure. Rather it is about groupmates who are not pulling their weight, who are taking too long to write their sections, who are unresponsive in group meetings, or who are just difficult to work with. Since they were in college, I had thought that they would be mature enough to resolve these conflicts. But I would almost always be dragged to a conversation about factions in research groups. Coming from this experience, I knew that one of the first things I had to do at the start of every term is to let students talk about what their expectations are of each other and how they plan to **handle group conflicts**.

There are different types of conflicts that can arise as people do their research. For students, there may be their groupmates who are free-riders. For professional researchers, there may be more contentious issues such as the proper framework or the differences in disciplinal perspectives. Some conflicts are because of people's quality of work while some are because of miscommunication or unaligned ideas. Whatever may be the cause of conflicts, it is important for groups to see how they can **talk about these conflicts** in an open atmosphere. Some groups will want to just sweep these items under the rug or just forego these conflicts. For some, this sweeping under the rug might be useful, but these little frustrations can boil and burst with just the smallest of inconveniences.

Before any conflicts arise, groups can talk about their expectations and their preferred ways of giving feedback to each other. **Expectations** are important so that groups are clear about deadlines, writing style, roles, delegated tasks, and communication channels. Setting and settling these things at the start of the research process can help groups have smoother interactions in the future. Another important thing to do is to clarify the ways one can give feedback to group members. Some people prefer to receive feedback personally rather than through e-mail while some would rather receive (or give) feedback without the face-to-face interaction. Whatever are people's preferred ways of receiving feedback, you will have to take note of it. Possibly more basic than preference is the clarity of why feedback must be given—and the assumption that when one gives feedback, these are done with the best of intentions. If you are working in groups, you will have to clarify why feedback is important and what good it brings to your group. Otherwise, feedback can easily turn into a source of resentment.

A more subtle source of conflict—and more so, an ethical concern—is the prevalence of gift and ghost authors. **Gift authors** are authors who are included in the byline but who have not made substantial contributions to the research while **ghost authors** are those who have contributed to the research but are not included in the research byline.[8] This can happen with research groups, collaborators, or advisers. To avoid this type of conflict, it is best to speak with people who have made contributions to your research and clarify authorship. The International Committee of Medical Journal Editors has a set of authorship criteria that includes:

> 1) substantial contributions to conception and design, or acquisition of data, or analysis and interpretation of data; 2) drafting the article or revising it critically for important intellectual content; and 3) final approval of the version to be published....
>
> Acquisition of funding, collection of data, or general supervision of the research group, alone, does not justify authorship.[9]

Although the above is for medical journals, it can be applied to other disciplines as well, where authorship is about making **significant contributions** to the different aspects of the research, from conception to publishing. Yet inasmuch as there are these broad guidelines, authorship is actually a debated and debatable topic among academics.[10] Thus, one must also know the disciplinary convention about the involvement of research advisers as co-authors in a paper. A good practice for this is to clarify authorship at the start of the research process rather than at the end when the paper is about to be submitted for publication.

1.6 Personal problems and emergencies

In this chapter about the research process, the focus has been on aspects of the research that you have control over: your time, the project's feasibility, following of guidelines, and ways of avoiding conflicts. However, things are not always within your control. Researchers encounter personal tragedies, family problems, financial constraints, mental health issues, and other concerns. During the course of your research (whether for a publication or a requirement), you may experience the loss of a loved one, an unanticipated crisis, a financial difficulty, or a bout of insecurity or depression. All these concerns are legitimate even if they may lead to your research taking the backseat.

When these difficulties come, there is no one particular way to solve them. However, I write them here so that you are not surprised or caught off-guard if these problems come. Problems—particularly those we have no control over—are natural, and you can actually think about how you plan to address these personal problems if they do arise. If there are particular events that you think are more likely to affect you (e.g. financial difficulties), it will be good to plan ahead on how to respond to these.

As emergencies arise, it will be best to **tell certain people** about this difficulty. If you are a student, it will be best to inform your research adviser about your situation since advisers usually find ways to help and support their students. They may not be able to provide financial or counseling support but they may be able to extend deadlines or find ways so that you can focus on your problem first rather than your research. If you are writing with a group, it will be a good idea to inform the group or your partner about your present situation (and do not feel the need to disclose all details). Letting them know your situation can help them understand if you are unable to concentrate on the research or if you need more time to finish certain things. You will also have to clarify what requests you will make of your adviser or research team.

Having these personal problems and emergencies does not necessarily mean that you will be unable to finish your research.

People have encountered adversities but were able to compartmentalize things and proceeded with their research as if they did not have these problems. A problem is neither a death sentence to your research nor an excuse for sloppy work. Honesty about your situation goes a long way and foreseeing emergencies can help you strategize how to address them if they do come.

CHAPTER 2
MISTAKES IN CONCEPTUALIZATION

The previous chapter focused on the common mistakes committed throughout the research process, whether from unclear purpose or because of one's inability to follow certain research procedures. This chapter focuses on the common mistakes made during the early parts of one's research—that is, as you conceptualize your research project. These could be mistakes in your research questions, which could actually be rooted in the lack of familiarity with the topic, or on your research argument, which could be totally unrelated to the question you initially had. Other mistakes common during the conceptualization phase are problems with structure (whether of the whole paper or of the literature review) and errors in the purpose of a literature review.

Aside from mentioning these common errors, the chapter provides practical and creative tips to address these mistakes before they happen. It outlines how you can create questions that are not too vague, too specific, or too narrow; it provides pointers on how to make arguments answer your question, and vice versa; it shows practical tips that help structure your literature review and clarify the review's purpose. By knowing these mistakes, you can think about how to work on conceptualizing your research so that your ideas and arguments can take center stage.

2.1 Lack of preliminary reading

One lament teachers have is that students **no longer read** books and long papers. With the advent of social media and news in the form of tweets, it is no surprise that the youth (including even a number of adults) would much prefer quick and immediate ideas rather than go through the process and difficulty of reading academic books, journal articles, and other scholarly writing. One reality that has affected this preference for short readings would be the ubiquity or the easy access to materials on the internet. It is much easier for people to read an internet "article" that they found on a Google search, and much more difficult to go to the library to search for the catalog number, go to the book shelf, look for the book, skim parts of the book, and type up the idea that you will borrow from the book. As you use your imagination, you will see that there is a huge difference in the amount of time needed to read internet articles and time needed for researching with library books.

But this trend of people unable to read lengthy and sustained arguments provides a great disservice to the research process. Although I do not discount the importance of a researcher's experience as a possible stimulus for a research question, I do think that much will be gained if researchers will be able to both **reflect** on experiences and **read** about how others have experienced these realities. At this point I am talking not about reading for a literature review but about reading to explore research topics and to focus your research question. Many people prefer already having a research question at the beginning without themselves being immersed in the ideas about their desired topic. But to have a good research question, it is important to be familiar with the broad strokes of the research topic. If you want to research on good management practices, it is not enough to ask "What are good management practices?" You will have to read up on what others have already written about the topic.

Doing **preliminary reading** is about reading for your research topic and question; it is not yet about the systematic ordering and critique of literature. Preliminary reading is about knowing the broad ideas that surround your research, immersing yourself in the vocabulary of a particular perspective, and understanding what are known and not yet known. One does not need to read everything about the topic at this stage, but it does help to read on both foundational and more current knowledge about your topic. If you wish, you can have a notebook to jot down your initial ideas but the more important task here is simply to read so that you can become familiar with what you want to research on.

If you are doing a study on suicide, it will be good to refer to Émile Durkheim's classic work, *Suicide: A Study in Sociology,* where he talks about the differences of egoistic, altruistic, and anomic suicide.[11] He argues that not all suicides are because of the person's feeling of being disconnected from other people. Rather there are some suicides that are altruistic—that is, they do this for a "higher purpose" as a means of sacrifice. Some suicides are also anomic—that is, caused by having too many apparent possibilities. More recent works on suicide by Anna Mueller and Seth Abrutyn take into consideration how close social knits can put pressure on individuals, and how these social bonds can actually lead to, rather than prevent, suicide ideation.[12] When you are **exposed to these different studies**, you are in a better position to craft your research question.

When conceptualizing a research project, one of the most common mistakes is to skip preliminary reading, and the only way to address this is by doing the reading yourself. I remember an old high school teacher being asked if it will be difficult to study in college, and his response was short but deeply penetrating: "There is no alternative to hard work." In a world where fast, quick, and easy answers are preferred, the way of hard work can often be old-fashioned. But the high school teacher—who has likely experienced anything from family problems to World War II—said something important: you just have to work hard.

2.2 Vague research questions

After doing your preliminary reading, you will be better able to craft your research question. However, even the best researchers can fall into the trap of writing vague research questions, or questions that are either too broad or too specific. Examples of research questions that are **too broad** are:

What are the most important environmental problems?
How do we create better policies?
Why do students cut classes?

From these research questions, you are not particularly sure how a researcher is able to answer these questions, or even how to define words such as "environmental problems" and "better" policies. Research questions will have to be grounded on particular, specific realities, but you must also be careful about being so specific that your research question becomes cases that are unique to the particular phenomenon without any broader implications. Some questions that border on **too specific** include:

What environmental problem is evident in the *estero* near Binondo?
How was the North Luzon Expressway created?
Why do third-year high school students in Negros High School cut English classes?

In these examples, it will be good to find a middle ground that is not too broad or too specific. It is important to have one foot on a **grounded phenomenon** that you are trying to study while at the same time have another foot on the **broader implications** and insights from the specific reality you are studying. If you plan to research on the environment, it might be good to ask what factors have contributed to water pollution in a village, and the insights can be extended since other villages have similar profiles. If you intend to study a government policy, you can ask about the principles used for a particular project, and how this applies to other contexts. If you will research on a particular school, you can question how students understand or make sense of their deviant behavior.

Another mistake that can happen with a tentative research question is to have these questions loaded with assumptions. A group of students asked if they can do a research on the ill effects of computer games, and the mistake here is that they are already assuming that computer games have ill effects. Thus, when writing your research question, you should ask what hidden assumptions you might have. Are you assuming that there is a cause and effect relationship? Are these assumptions justified? Are there research articles that dispute your assumptions?[13] It is important and safer to explore questions that are neutral at the start, such as asking how mobile games influence students' study habits or how computer games affect memory retention. In these questions, there are no assumptions of whether they have good or ill effects, nor are there assumptions of causal relationships.

As you do research, you must expect that your research question will have many iterations since you will have to refine, distill, and specify the issue. It is also important to note that the research question is tentative and temporary, and can change with the inclusion of more data and information. So why not just wait for all data to be there and craft the question after? Having a tentative research question at the start is still important so that you do not waste time with getting data that you will likely not need in the future.

2.3 Unidentified research gap

When you already have your research question, you do not yet immediately perform your research or experiment. You will first have to clarify (first for yourself and then for your reader) what is the **gap in our knowledge**. What are things that we do not know about the phenomenon, its causes or its effects? What have others already investigated and what is left to investigate? What new things can we say about the thing we will research on? Clearly, the mistake is to not clarify this gap at the beginning of the research.

In medical experiments that test if a drug is effective, one criterion for research is **equipoise**, or the point where there is "no preference between treatments, i.e., it is thought equally likely that treatment A or B will turn out to be superior."[14] This means that there is room to doubt if a particular treatment, or specifically medicine, will be more effective than another treatment or having no treatment at all. To think of this more generally, equipoise is about seeing if there is still room for us to doubt the conclusions from our research. It is to see if there is indeed a gap in knowledge that we are addressing. If other people cannot doubt our argument, this may mean that the argument has already been settled. Researching on the ill effects of smoking may not be adding anything new to the body of knowledge because this is already generally accepted.

When doing research, however, you must show the significance by talking about how the answer to your question is not obvious. You will have to show that there is something **original** in your argument, or that at least your argument **nuances** the insights from another research. By the term nuance, I mean that your argument should provide an added perspective to what is generally known to be true. To say that basketball is one of the most popular sports in the Philippines does not merit much original thinking; it is a self-evident fact. However, to argue that basketball has been used as a means of colonizing and pacifying the Philippines is an interesting and debatable argument.[15] In this way, the latter argument shows originality in thinking and addresses a particular gap in research.

If you plan to do research and have it published, it is important to identify what the gap in the knowledge is and how your research addresses it. Failure to show how your research addresses a knowledge gap may lead to your finding out similar things that other people already know. It is also important to note how clarifying your research gap can help you focus your research ideas. Similar to the ideas in Chapter 1, knowing your purpose for undertaking a research—that is, the gap you are addressing—can help you determine which are essential for your research.

2.4 Unclear hypothesis or argument

After clarifying your research question and research gap, you may be tempted to create a survey or interview people already. It is a common misconception that you only need to have a research question and can already proceed with the research proper. However, this type of thinking can lead to a research that is **vague** at best and **uncoordinated** at worst. After having a sense of the scholarly field, it will be helpful to have a working hypothesis or a tentative argument. A **hypothesis** is a testable statement about how variables are related, and this is particularly helpful in quantitative research.[16] Since it is testable, you will have to show and test whether a hypothesis is true or false. Its usual formulation is in "If a.., then b...", which means that if a certain condition holds true, the other condition also holds true. A simplified example of a hypothesis is:

> If a student attends a tutorial for college exams, he is more likely to be accepted.

In this type of research, you will have to see if those who attend tutorial classes are more likely to be accepted in college than those who do not. Thus, you will need two groups (one that went to tutorial and the other that did not) and you will have to obtain the percentage of those who were accepted in each group. By comparing these two percentages (through analysis of variance—which will be discussed in Chapter 3), you will see if your hypothesis holds true.

Similarly, one can also have a **null hypothesis**, which states that there is no relationship between or among the variables in your study.[17] In the previous example, we were trying to test if "going to tutorial classes" (variable A) affected "college acceptance" (variable B). For a null hypothesis, we assume that variable A and variable B are not related to each other, and so we can phrase our hypothesis (H_1) and null hypothesis (H_0) as:

> H_1: There is a positive relationship between going to tutorials and college acceptance.
> H_0: There is no relationship between going to tutorials and college acceptance.

We can prove the null hypothesis if we see there were similar percentages of college acceptance for both those who went to tutorial classes and those who did not. Admittedly, though, this is an oversimplified version since there may be bias in the sample, which is to say that those who had tutorials may have certain characteristics (like being grade-conscious or having a higher socioeconomic status) that are different from those who did not go to tutorials.

For qualitative research, it will be good to have a qualified guess or **tentative argument** at the start of your research. What is your tentative answer to your research question? How do you think your research respondents will respond to your research? What are reasons behind your tentative argument? If your research question is about what factors help students get accepted to exclusive colleges, you may tentatively say that practicing for entrance tests, performing well in senior high school, and getting good recommendation letters all contribute to being accepted in college. This can form part of your tentative research argument. In this way, you will know what more to ask from your respondents and how to deepen your understanding of their answers.

When working with a tentative research argument, you will also be more sensitive and deliberate about where to find your **reasons** and **evidence**. Having a sense of what your argument will be about, you will know whom to contact, what to ask them, and how to deepen your knowledge of the phenomenon you are studying.

2.5 Unaligned Question and Argument

A research group wanted to investigate how male and female student-athletes are perceived similarly or differently from each other. As they did their research and conducted their interviews, they realized that college student-athletes were sometimes admired by their classmates while at the same time were judged as lazy or perceived as receiving special treatment from professors. It was an interesting research, and there were a lot of insights from their interviews of both student-athletes and regular students. However, when they were asked about how male and female athletes experienced these perceptions differently, they were unable to account for this. They focused so much on the perception that they forgot that their research was about the difference between male and female student-athletes.

This is a classic mistake of the research argument **not answering the initial research question**, and this is a common occurrence. Sometimes because of the ways things progress and because of new insights that come during your research, you can lose sight of your initial research question. When faced with this problem and you still have time to gather information, it will be good to go back to your research question and see how that can be answered with the data you have.

However, if you have no more time to do further research or if you feel that this new direction is what you ultimately wanted to pursue, it may be good for you to **change your research question** into one that more closely aligns with the answers you currently have. It may seem absurd that you will change your question based on the answers that you get (as if this was a game of Jeopardy) but this actually shows how the research process is not always linear and sequential. There are times when you will have to change your research design and question even if the research has already begun.[18] What is important is that your research question and argument are aligned.

In order to address this, it will be a good idea to periodically check how your current research aligns with or matches your original research question. One way of doing this is by asking the research question first and seeing if your thesis statement matches your question. For example, if you ask what *factors* affected the rise of populism but most of your research is about the *effects* of populism, then your research argument does not match your question, and you will have to clarify what you want addressed specifically in your research. Showing the connection between your question and argument is important so that your readers do not lose focus.

2.6 Unclear research structure

One beginning researcher structured her research in this way:

> This research will begin with a discussion of the things I've read… After reading these materials, I consulted with an expert and then created an interview guide for the people I will interview… Since I needed to interview ten people, I called three people to ask if they can participate, and they said they can participate. They know of another person who wanted to participate so I interviewed this person also. After four days, I was able to complete my interviews.

> After this, I typed the interviews and saw what were the common threads in the research... The common threads were about... At the end of the research, I conclude that...[19]

In this example, we see how methodical the author was. Although this shows how much effort and meticulousness went into her research, this methodical way of conveying the research is not the preferred structure in the exposition of research.

Although research in the humanities will have more fluidity in the components, there is often an expected structure in empirical papers in the natural, social, and applied sciences. These papers traditionally follow the **IMRAD structure**, or the Introduction, Methods, Results and Discussion. Although the research structure is not as tidy and linear as this structure provides, it does enable the reader to quickly scan and locate different parts of the paper for information.[20]

The *introduction* usually provides the research question and objective as well as the review of relevant literature. This first section tells the reader about what is known and unknown about this research question. The second section on the *methods* talks about how the researchers obtained and analyzed their data while the third section on *results* shows the processed insights from the collected data (whether through surveys, interviews, or other means). The last section on *discussion*, which can include the conclusion, usually interprets what the raw results mean and tells the reader how these results answer the broad research question. This last section also informs readers about how the present research connects with other studies.

Although the IMRAD structure is the convention, there are really just two things that are set: the introduction at the start and the conclusion at the end. Most of the other things in the middle can shift and move around, but if you plan to veer from the IMRAD model, it may be a good idea to talk about your **research structure** at the beginning of your research. Since you are going against the convention, it is best to inform and guide your reader how to read your research.

Part of your task as researcher will be to **organize** and **communicate** what you know about your research to your audience. On the one hand, you should not feel boxed into a singular structure like the IMRAD structure; on the other hand, you will have to consider how you can help the reader make sense of your research. To enumerate the twists and turns of your research may not be very effective in conveying your ideas. To list your ideas chronologically as they came to you may be good for a personal journal entry, but not for a scientific journal that asks you to consolidate knowledge. Thus, you will have to clarify and be deliberate about how you structure your research.

2.7 Undefined terms

Here are examples of sentences that some researchers would write in the first paragraphs of their thesis or article:

> CHED has given a lot of scholarships to professors...
> People who experience chronic spontaneous urticaria have difficulties...
> Intelligent people often get into exclusive schools...

In these examples, the mistakes are concentrated in how particular terms are used in the research. For the first example, the term "CHED" should have been defined first. Some people in the Philippines might know what CHED means but there may be someone from Vietnam who will read your paper and will need to know what the acronym means. Thus, you will have to **write out the acronym** and even have to say something about the agency or the institution first. You will have to write both "Commission on Higher Education (CHED)" and a short description of what CHED does. In other words, it is necessary for acronyms to be spelled out during the first instance of use and for particular agencies and institutions to be described briefly in the beginning section of your research.

In the second example, the unfamiliar term "chronic spontaneous urticaria" is not defined for general readers. When you are about to introduce a technical term to your reader, you should be sure to define this at the start of your research and not wait until the literature review. In this case, you can talk briefly in the introduction about how *chronic spontaneous urticaria* is a skin condition in which the person experiences hives or allergies almost daily for at least six weeks.[21] You can then talk about other aspects of this skin condition in your literature review.

It is understandable, however, that since you are immersed in the literature and are an expert in an area, you forget that some words you use are new and foreign to other people. Thus, one quick fix to this is by asking a person who is not from your discipline to quickly scan your paper and see **what terms need to be clarified** or defined earlier. These new words may also be geographic or cultural, not only technical. For example, I wrote a paper on in-school suspensions, and even if this is usual in the United States, this was not at all done in the Philippines and other developing countries so I knew I had to define this term at the start of my research.[22] Similarly, one culture may have appropriated terms for daily use (like dreadlocks or reggae), which will have to be defined as well.

In the third example on "intelligent people," the mistake is that we do not know how the word *intelligent* was defined. How do we measure intelligence? Is this the same as having high scores in an exam? It is easy for researchers to use words that are ill-defined like intelligence, which makes it all the more important to **operationalize terms**. This operationalization means defining concepts in terms of quantifiable observations or measurements.[23]

When you talk about intelligence, you will have to specify if you are trying to measure it in terms of IQ (or intelligent quotient), examination grades, or school performance. When you talk about poverty, you will have to operationalize or define it: does it mean earning less than a particular amount of money per day? an individual's salary or the family's combined salary? the family's earnings or the family's spending? Aside from intelligence and poverty, other common terms that need operationalization include children/youth (below 18, 21, or 30?), higher achievement (college, masters, or doctoral degrees?), or better company results (overall sales, employee loyalty, or customer satisfaction?). Particularly when you do a quantitative study, you will have to carefully define and operationalize your terms at the beginning parts of your research so that your reader will know what you are talking about.

This mistake of being unable to define (whether acronyms, technical words, or harder-to-measure concepts) is quite common, particularly for someone immersed in the research community, literature, or process. But this can also be easily fixed by reading the paper with fresh eyes—whether these eyes are borrowed from someone else, or you yourself will deliberately look for vague terms that need to be clarified.

2.8 Literature reviews as book or article summaries

One of the more difficult tasks of a researcher is to do a literature review since this means searching for articles, books, and ideas that align with your research question. Because of this difficulty, beginning research students tend to think that if they find an article connected to their research, they can immediately just write a **paragraph summary** of this article or book, and this will make up one part of their literature review. A research student may also feel that a literature review is about finding relevant articles and just writing down salient facts about what was already said. It thus becomes a hodgepodge of ideas that relate to the research.

However, a literature review is not a collection of book or article summaries. One of the most helpful ways to talk about literature review is to separate the process from the product of the review. In terms of the **process**, literature review happens when you pick up (or Google search) and read materials for your research. You read them and write notes about basic concepts, questions, ideas, and new discoveries. This process is about knowing how people have thought and debated about your research topic—and part of your role is to help organize what is already known about the topic. It is this organization part that people find more challenging, and the next section talks about how to create a coherent literature review or introduction.

In terms of **product**, the literature review is a written document that provides what is known and not known about the topic in an effort to show how your research adds or fits in this ecosystem of what is known and unknown. A good definition of this review is provided by Chris Hart, who defines it as:

> the selection of available documents (both published and unpublished) on the topic, which contain information, ideas, data, and evidence written from a particular standpoint to fulfill certain aims and express certain views on the nature of the topic and how it is to be investigated, and the effective evaluation of these documents in relation to the research being proposed.[24]

In this definition of literature review, I highlight how there are three main aims of a literature review: to express a view on a topic, to know how it can be investigated, and to evaluate these published and unpublished works in relation to the present research project. Nowhere in this definition does it say that the literature review should summarize books or articles.

Thus, when doing the review, you must show how these written works can be organized to show your **particular stance** on a topic. Do you agree with what is generally known or do you disagree with it? Is there a debate or uncertainty in the field that you wish to clarify with your research? Do you plan to use a theory on a particular situation? In the end, your stance will be influenced by what research question you have. At the end of the literature review, you will have to show how your present research adds to, confirms, or challenges what is already known about the topic.

Additionally, writing a literature review does not mean that you only have to agree with what others have already said. An important part of the review is also **challenging** what is generally known. You have to show that you have read so widely on the topic that you can critique others' ideas. This critical stance towards research is about criticizing not the author but the lapses of particular written documents. You can talk about how the paper does not document for a particular population, how the paper is not generalizable, or how there was a particular flaw with the research method. By carefully challenging certain ideas, you can show how your research tries to address these concerns.

So remember, the literature review is not a summary section of what others have written. You will have to organize and systematize what is known about the topic, and in order to do this effectively you will have to read widely on your topic. A common mistake is thinking that reading two or three articles will be enough to write a literature review. Although there is no prescribed number of books or articles to read, reading fewer than five articles will not serve your research well. You will have to learn more about your topic and how others are discussing it. Searching for resources is so much easier now with the Internet, Google Scholar, Google Books, and many other technologies at your disposal. In addition to this access, there has also been so much more information that it is unacceptable to say that you did not find enough literature on your topic.

2.9 Incoherent literature review

Now that you know a literature review is supposed to provide a way of introducing your research topic—why it is significant, what are outstanding debates, and how other researchers have viewed your topic—a further mistake made by beginning researchers is **failing to structure** the ideas in a literature review. Some literature reviews seem to jump from one topic to another without any coherent structure. Thus, this section hopes to offer some helpful guides and principles in writing a more coherent literature review.

Clarity in writing comes when there is **clarity in thinking**, so one of the first things you will have to do as you write your literature review is to clarify the main argument. For research proposals, you will have to write the literature review first before doing the actual research or experiments. In this type of research, you will have to clarify the intellectual debates and uncertainties, and how your research will fill the gap in the knowledge. For research articles published in journals, some authors prefer writing the introduction and literature review only after they have done the experiments. In this way, they want to have a solid understanding of the phenomenon, and then provide the background with which the insights can be couched. With this process, you will know which research findings to include and how you will package the research gap because you are already clear about your contribution.

Whether you are to write the literature review at the start of your research or at the end of it, it is best to have an outline of the **broad topics** you wish to engage. If you are writing a paper on factors that affect teachers' use of computer-assisted instruction, you can talk broadly about (1) different educational technologies, (2) positive and negative effects of these technologies, and (3) teachers' perception of technology in the classroom. When you have these broad topics, think about how you will structure your review such that it follows the path of your argument. Some examples are:

- **Topical** structure involves dividing your literature into particular clusters that only need natural logic. For example, a research on education reform can have three parts: basic education, vocational education, and higher education reforms.
- **Compare and contrast** structure involves organizing your review in such a way that you show the similarities and differences between particular studies. For example, a research on the Filipinos' reception of K-pop and J-pop can include the similarities of these two pop groups as well as their differences.
- **Advantages and disadvantages/ agreement and disagreement** structure involves showing two sides of a particular argument, and how there are still outstanding debates about them. For example, a research on the use of artificial intelligence (AI) can show studies that are for the use of AI and those that are against the use of AI.
- **Order of importance** structure involves moving either from the most important aspects of the study to the least important, or from the least important to the most important. It can also be from the broadest significance to the most specific ones. For example, a research on language education reform can start by showing the literature on education reform in general, and then move to national education reforms in the Philippines, and then focus on education reforms on language curriculum. In this example, it moves from the broadest to the most specific.
- **Chronological** or **sequential** structure involves providing the steps that an idea has gone through, whether historically or

thematically. You should be careful when using this type of structure because of how it might end up like a storytelling of the intellectual knowledge rather than a solid literature review. For example, research on a medicine can include the chronological discussion of how the medicine came to be.

- **Factors** structure involves presenting research on the factors that have influenced a particular phenomenon. For example, a literature review on college cheating can have studies on the factors that influence cheating: peer expectations, parental pressure, difficult exams, etc.
- **Problem and solution** structure involves showing how a particular problem has been addressed or fixed by different solutions. For example, a research on rural poverty can have literature about the different tested solutions like conditional cash transfer, livelihood programs, and so on.[25]

These are just some ways that could inspire you to think about the structure of your literature review and encourage you to develop other ways of structuring the literature review, depending on the study you have at hand.

After knowing the structure of your literature review, you can find studies within the topics you wanted to cover. As you look for these studies and research papers, you should take note of the differences and the gaps in what these studies have previously researched. Remember that you not only have to tell your reader about the study but also have to evaluate or critique the studies. You will have to talk about the research findings of a particular research, how this is shared by other researchers, and how this is connected to your present study. Similarly, there may be other researchers who do not agree with the research you first saw. When this happens, it will be your task to show the probable reasons why there have been inconsistent findings.[26]

Another practical tip for helping with the structure of your literature review (particularly for long reviews) is to provide an **overview** at the beginning of your review. For instance:

> In this literature review, I first discuss the advent of different educational technologies. After this discussion, I map out how

their positive and negative effects are evident in public schools. Lastly, I focus on how these effects could affect teachers' perception and use of computer-assisted instruction.

By stating at the start how the next few paragraphs will be structured, you are providing your audience with a reading blueprint. It will also be a good idea to **use subheadings** so that the reader will again be able to trace back and structure what you are saying in your review.

In the same way that you have an overview at the beginning of your research, you should also aim at having a conclusion that summarizes the most important insights in the literature and how this connects with what you are currently studying. By summarizing the important insights, you are showing why your research is important and how it can add to our knowledge.

2.10 Outdated or unreliable literature

In one research class, a research group relied on just five books for their literature review, and one book they referred to was published in 1926! Although there is nothing wrong with consulting the classics on a topic, **failure to provide up-to-date research, findings,** and **examples** can actually signal either that the topic has already been settled or studied to death, or that the researcher is not familiar with the more recent developments on the topic. Either way, it will not be a good idea to rely solely on old research.

It will be your task to see and scour for what others have recently said about your topic. Some research advisers would advise finding sources within the last ten years while some will advise even more recent ones. Although there is no set rule as to how recent your literature sources should be, it is important to be deliberate about your choice of current and classic literature, combining the **foundational knowledge** of the classics and the nuances presented by **contemporary findings**. In some studies, researchers start with the classic approach and add more recent writers who have enhanced or challenged the classic research findings. Using more recent findings also helps show how the topic is still understood given present-day issues and concerns.[27]

To find more recent publications, you can search for papers and books in **more scholarly search websites**: Jstor, EBSCO-Host, Google Books, Google Scholar, Elsevier, Sage Publications, Taylor and Francis Journals, Routledge, and so on. By using these search engines (rather than your typical Google search), you also address another common research mistake: using unreliable sources. Teachers and research advisers would usually lament how the literature review is infused with web articles and is almost devoid of books or journal papers. This is probably not because there is a dearth of books or journals but because of the habit of relying almost exclusively on Google for any search or "research." By changing your preferred browser from Google to Google Scholar, you may get more reliable information.

By doing your literature review search with these scholarly search engines, you limit your sources to more **credible articles** that have been peer-reviewed and published. The peer-review process ensures that other scholars and researchers vouch for the findings of a particular research, and this means that the paper achieves a level of reliability not seen with web articles that can be posted by anyone with an Internet access.[28] Thus, it is best to be deliberate in your literature search and look for papers that are recent, reliable, and reviewed by other scholars since these form the foundation of your research.

2.11 Unclear differentiation of framework and literature review

There can be many different ideas in a literature review, and one of the difficulties is that there may not be a structure that holds them all together. This is why some research studies require not only a literature review but also a framework that helps make sense of the things you are studying. It is about seeing how the different pieces fit together and how ideas relate with each other.[29] Now, if a framework is like this, how is it any different from a literature review that itself needs to be structured?

There are many debates here, and one perspective is that the terms *literature review, theoretical framework,* and *conceptual framework* are actually interchangeable. There is this idea because they all generally function in the same way as they provide a foundation for the research, and help the researcher **conceptualize the study** and **identify knowledge gaps**.[30] It will be noted that most journal articles will have just one section on either the literature review or the framework. However, there are also research projects—like theses and dissertations—where you need to have different sections for the literature review and the framework. Thus, here are some salient differences among the three:

- **Literature review** involves showing how others have studied and what others have discovered about a particular topic. It is like casting a net on an area that you want to explore in and showing the major authors, classic ideas, and current insights into the topic. The literature review is more focused on the topics and empirical studies rather than on the coherent theory or concepts that are tied together.
- **Theoretical framework** involves the presentation of a particular theory (usually showing how particular factors or variables affect or influence each other) and the empirical studies that support or challenge the theory. It is like a scaffolding that holds together your whole study, and this is most common for quantitative research where a theory is being proven or disproven. For this, there must first be an explanation of the theory and the framework shows how others have investigated this theory.
- **Conceptual framework** involves organizing the main ideas in your research and providing the network of relationships between them. Rather than have a set theory, it uses concepts and relationships between concepts, and shows how previous empirical studies try to advance these concepts. It is more like a map that shows how different aspects are related to each other.[31]

In summary, although they function similarly, these three introductory sections of the research have some slight differences. A **literature review** shows studies on a particular topic without need for theory or conceptual map, while a **framework** provides a structure or way of connecting ideas through either a theory or a web of conceptual relations.

Just one important idea to remember is that if you do use a theoretical or a conceptual framework, it is important for you to go back to the framework when you discuss your research. It will be unwise to leave your framework in the beginning part of your research but not talk about it during your discussion. This mistake happens when you have abandoned your theories or concepts and have not related them to the ideas you have uncovered. Thus, make it a point to say how the theoretical or conceptual framework is supported, challenged, or nuanced by your research.

CHAPTER 3

MISTAKES IN METHODS AND INSTRUMENTS

After knowing enough of the literature on your topic and after conceptualizing your research question, you will have to collect and gather data. In empirical research studies, you should not only rely on what others have already said; you will have to get the information yourself from a variety of sources and people. A common misconception about research is that it is just about organizing an argument from the various readings or previous research you have had. Some students would just read three or four sources and write a "research" that integrates the ideas from these articles or books. In this type of research, the person relies solely on second-hand data. However, research involves getting their own firsthand data. Researching is not about searching Google for an answer and stringing the insights together.

When doing research in the natural sciences, you will have to perform experiments; in the social sciences you will have to interview people or create surveys; in the humanities you will have to engage with a theory, a text, or a cultural artifact; in history you will have to use written or photographed materials; in market research you will have to do focus group discussions. In the different fields, you will have to obtain data for you to analyze, interpret, and make sense of.

In this chapter, we focus on common mistakes in the **collection**, **preparation**, **ethical execution**, and **analysis** of your research. There are mistakes when creating your research instruments and mistakes when doing the actual data collection of surveying or interviewing. Some include lapses when one does not comply with ethical standards or when data analysis is unclear. In this chapter, we look at what these mistakes are and how they can be avoided or addressed. Although the principles are general, there are some that apply better to quantitative studies while others that are more applicable for qualitative studies.

3.1 Inappropriate research method

Because of certain school requirements or subjects, some students use a method that is totally unrelated to the research question. Since you might be required a paper for a quantitative or qualitative methods class, you may think that it will be wise and efficient to ask the same research question. However, quantitative and qualitative studies have very different assumptions and focus.

For **quantitative research**, you are more interested in understanding the magnitude of phenomena or the causal patterns behind them. To know the prevalence of obesity in a particular region, one does not need to have qualitative interviews asking people how significant they think this phenomenon is. It is more important to do a survey with weight and eating behaviors as questions. For **qualitative research**, you are more interested in knowing the meaning or perception of particular phenomena. To know how Filipinos ascribe meaning to their food practices, it adds little help to do a quantitative survey of what food people eat. It is much more necessary to interview people about their meaning making for food. Thus, you will have to think carefully about the connection between your research question and your desired research method.

Sometimes, you will be required to follow a particular method because of a class (e.g. statistics or qualitative methods). If this happens, you should think about a research question that suits the method you learned. If you learned how to do inferential statistics, you will have to write a research question with dependent and independent variables.[32] If you are learning qualitative methods in a class, you will have to consider a question that looks at a person or a group's context and understanding of a particular phenomenon, event, or idea.[33] In either way, you will have to learn how to transform your research question such that you are using the method prescribed in a class.

However, there will also be times when you are given the freedom to use whatever method at your disposal. At times when you already have a research question, you will have to find a research method and design that fits your question. Is your research about quantifying or seeing patterns, or is it about finding meaning and identifying contexts? Does your research ask for a large population's preferences, or about a specific population's meaning making? Is your research asking closed-ended or open-ended questions? Do the research projects in your topic use mostly quantitative or qualitative methods? Do you plan to follow or challenge this trend? These are among the questions that you will have to ask as you try to ascertain your research method. You should know that there are also **mixed-methods approaches** where you can combine quantitative and qualitative methods to answer your research question. In these cases, you will have to use both research approaches.

When you have decided which method to use, you will have to create your **research design**, or the "set of formal procedures for collecting, analyzing, and interpreting data such as those found in quantitative experiment or qualitative case study."[34] Your research design is essentially your plan or strategy for investigating your research question. Among the most important principles is for your research design to flow directly from your research question. One of the most common mistakes committed is when the research strategies used have no connection at all to the original research question. For example, suppose your main research question is about Filipinos' food preferences according to socioeconomic status. In the survey you create, you ask your respondents about their favorite food and why they prefer this type of food. However, you did not ask anything about your respondents' socioeconomic position. In this case, your research design will be unable to answer your research question.

To address this mistake, you will have to ask if the answer you obtain in your research design will provide you with the **answers to your main research question**. If it does not, you have to reconsider your research design. It is also not just about creating the right questions in your survey or your interview. A good part of your research design is about knowing how you will use and interpret the data you obtain. To make this more concrete, you will have to first see if the questions you ask in your survey or interview are relevant to or match your primary research question. Second, you will have to show how the answers can be analyzed and interpreted, and how this interpretation links back to your research question.[35]

3.2 Sampling mistakes

When you do a research, you need not give everyone a survey or interview all the people involved in a community. A significant part of doing a research is about getting information from a group of people, not necessarily every single individual. This is what is often called a **sample**, or the subset of a particular population relevant for your study.[36] For example, in your research about interuniversity basketball in the UAAP (University Athletics Association of the Philippines), you do not need all students in the eight schools to answer your survey. It will be enough to have a representative sample from each of the eight schools.

The common mistake, however, is not that you get information from so many respondents but that you get information from **very few**. Of course, there will be differences in how this is done in qualitative and quantitative studies. For qualitative studies that involve observations or interviews, few respondents that provide **in-depth information** is perfectly fine. For these types of research, there is the concept of **data saturation**, where there is already a conceptual density or completeness in the information you have received from your informants.[37] Some scholars suggest that if other informants repeat the answers and there are no more new insights, this could hint at data saturation. In this way, the concern is not about the sample being representative of the population but about providing rich data that answers the research question. Here are examples of **non-probability sampling** for qualitative research:

- **Intensity sampling** usually consists of small sample sizes where participants are interviewed multiple times in order to get rich information.

- **Snowball sampling** involves getting participants through the referral of other participants; this is usually done in difficult-to-access populations.
- **Exemplary or negative case** consists of participants who are unusual for a particular group—cases like dramatic successes or failures, those that so clearly exhibit the phenomenon, or those who are the exact opposite.[38]
- **Purposive sampling** involves the researcher's inclusion of participants based on particular characteristics that match the objectives of the study.
- **Convenience sampling** is based on the convenient availability and proximity of the participants to the researcher.

When working with quantitative research, you will have to clarify the optimal number of respondents. If you have too many respondents and they answered surveys on paper, you will have a hard time encoding the data. This can also have cost implications. If you have too few, you will have a hard time being conclusive about your research results since your sample may not be representative. The results may be driven less by the phenomenon and more by the fact that the small sample answered things in a particular way. For example, a research on feelings about basketball answered by just ten of your close friends may lead you to think that 90% of students love basketball but this may be due to the fact that most of your friends like the game (well, at least nine out of your ten friends do).

In terms of representativeness in quantitative studies, it is important to be intentional about the sample you plan to have in your research. There are different ways of representative probability sampling or getting a group that accurately reflects the larger population with members of a population having equal chances (probability) of being included. Here are some ways of doing **probability sampling**:

- In **simple random sampling,** selection is only a matter of chance. Thus, each person will have an equal chance as everyone else to be included.
- In **stratified sampling,** each smaller group of a population

will be used as a stratum (e.g. *barangays* for a larger city) and the researcher will select from each stratum, noting the size of each group and applying this to the number of people selected (e.g. a larger barangay will have more respondents in a survey). In this type of research, you will have to get a proportionate number of respondents from every barangay in the city.

- In **cluster sampling,** a population is divided into separate groups called clusters and the researcher will select a random sample of clusters. In this research, you will only have to select possibly two or three barangays that will be the clusters for your research.[39]

As you do your research, it will be important to clarify the type of sampling you plan to use and whether you will use probability or non-probability samples. One thing that you just have to guard against is the potential sources of bias when you have limited your survey respondents or interview participants to those who share your ideas or those who have similar ideas with each other.

Another mistake that relates with sampling is when you do not clarify the people who should be included or excluded in your study, whether qualitative or quantitative. Clarifying your **inclusion and exclusion criteria** is extremely important when doing your research since this is your way of defining your population of interest.[40] For a research on mothers, it will be important to exclude those who are male, and women who have not yet given birth. For a research on computer games, a necessary inclusion criterion may be that these people should be playing computer games for at least eight hours every week. For a research on undergraduate students, you will have to clarify that the only criterion for inclusion is that one is studying in college; there should consequently be no other exclusions based on gender, sexual orientation, regional birthplace, or socioeconomic status. Whether in qualitative or quantitative study, the standards for a person's inclusion or exclusion from the study should be clarified at the start of the research.

3.3 Erroneous survey questionnaires

When you clarify your research approach and respondents, you will have to create your research instruments, whether this be a survey questionnaire for quantitative studies or an interview/observation guide for qualitative studies. In this section, we focus on how **inaccurate survey questionnaires** can affect your results and the conclusions you draw from these results. In research, there is the concept of trash in trash out, which means that unscrupulous researchers who may unknowingly obtain "garbage" answers will themselves likely write research that do not accurately portray what is being studied. Oftentimes, we get these types of answers because the questions we ask are incorrect or inaccurate, or we do not get to ask the questions that needed to be asked of participants. The mistake comes not from the people you collect data from, but from the very instrument used for collecting data.

When using questionnaires, you can use instruments that have already been used, or particular psychological tests that are already internally valid. Alternatively, you can create your own tests to suit your research question. If you must create your own test, it will be a good idea to ask experts about their opinions, interview target respondents to ascertain which questions to ask on the test, and do a pilot study before rolling out the whole survey instrument. Sometimes, one's constructed research instrument can be peppered with mistakes because of how researchers think that they just need to write logical questions. However, there is a certain science and art to creating these instruments.

For example, a researcher wants to find out how parents' attitudes on schooling affect the outcomes of their senior high school child. In this shortened sample questionnaire given to parents, try to assess what mistakes are present:

Name of Parent: Name of Child:

(1.1) Parent's details:
Highest educational attainment:
Sex:
Average salary:
(1.2) Student's details:
Grade:

Tuition: 10,000
20,000
30,000

(2.1) On a scale of 1 to 5, how important is school?

(2.2) We heard that attendance is a problem in your school. Is your child attending school?

(2.3) Why do some children perform well in their studies and why do some cause a lot of trouble?

In this short survey form, you may have seen a couple of glaring mistakes already, and we will discuss a number of these mistakes and how to prevent them. First, you will notice that the names of the parents and child are asked in this survey. One of the things that you will have to protect with your research respondents is their identity and the **confidentiality** of their data. Thus, unless the name is essential to the study, it will be best to let respondents answer surveys **anonymously**. They may be given code numbers and these codes can just be linked through a protected file so as to ensure confidentiality.

In question 1.1 on the parent's detail, the parent will have to write his or her highest educational attainment, gender, and average salary. Although this is alright, it will be difficult to recode handwritten data. For example, parents who have graduated from college may write on the space: (1) college, (2) undergraduate, (3) university graduate, (4) college grad, etc. Although they all refer to the same thing, the way they wrote about it is different from each other. Thus, it will be helpful to provide your respondents with **choices** such as:

Highest educational degree attained: No high school attainment
High school graduate
College graduate
Master's graduate
PhD/ MD/ Law graduate

In this way, it will be easy for your respondent to answer and even easier for you to code and analyze your data. Similarly, you can write

Male and Female as options for Sex. For average salary, aside from providing options, you also have to clarify the **time frame** and the **scope.** Is it average salary for the month or the year? Is it the average individual salary, the average salary of the couple, or the average salary of all those working in a household? Since salaries can be quite variable, you will have to provide **ranges** in the option, and also an option of "Above #" if your range is limited. For example:

Average individual monthly salary: PHP 0 - 20,000
PHP 20,001 - 40,000
PHP 40,001 - 60,000
PHP 60,001 - 80,000
....
Above PHP 200,000

By doing this, it is easier for you to see if there are patterns in your respondents' answers. For the student's detail, it will also be good to clarify what "Grade" means. Does it mean the grade in school, like 10th or 12th grade? Does it mean the grade for a particular subject? Does it mean the Grade Point Average (GPA)? If it is the GPA, is it for the semester, the whole year, or the whole stay during senior high school? This will again be open to a lot of interpretation, and so it is important to change this to "Grade Point Average Last Semester" if one is interested to show the student's most recent performance.

All of these emphasize the importance of getting **demographic information** about the people who participate in your research. You can create categories providing salient differentiation between different groups. For example, you may want categories for the students' tracks in senior high school to see if there are people from particular tracks that are performing better on average. When working on the survey, it will also help if you are familiar with the types of questions to ask:

1. **Selected response format** means that the respondent answers from a set of choices available.
2. **Dichotomous format** is a selected response where there are two options: yes/no or true/false.

3. **Polytomous format** is a selected response where there are more than two options.
4. **Single response** means that the respondent is forced to answer only one from a given set of options (e.g. Male or Female).
5. **Multiple response** means that the respondent can answer more than one, or none at all. (e.g. Which countries have you visited in the last 2 years?)
6. **Ranking** means that you are forced to put in order a given set of options.
7. **Rating** means that you have to evaluate and give a score on every item.

One of the most common examples of doing a rating in a survey is with **Likert scale ratings** where you evaluate a statement on your agreement or disagreement with it. For example, one can have a statement like "Education is important to me" and have options such as *Strongly agree, Agree, Neutral, Disagree, Strongly disagree.* This could have been a better way of asking the first question in the sample survey, the one which only asked "On a scale of 1 to 5, how important is school?" In the original question, what do the 1 to 5 mean anyway? How can my 4 be distinguished from someone else's 3? When one uses a Likert scale, there is a qualitative distinction between strong agreement and just simple agreement. Of course, this is not a perfect tool but it is far better than just arbitrarily asking one's rating on a scale of 1 to 5.

Some issues to consider when using Likert scales include determining the **number of options** and having **midpoints**. Usually, a Likert scale has five or seven options, which are often coded 1 to 5, or 1 to 7. Sometimes, there are six options with the midpoint changed to *Somewhat agree* and *Somewhat disagree* to avoid a person conveniently using *Neutral* for uncritical or unmotivated respondents. Nonetheless, midpoints can be helpful for people who genuinely feel neutral about a topic. Whether you choose five or six options, you should at least make sure that the options are consistent across the research instrument.

In some surveys, there will be questions that cannot be easily grouped in a selected response format (closed-ended responses). At these points, you will have to create open-ended questions that provide for broader answers. With these kinds of questions, there are two mistakes that you have to be careful with: leading questions and double-barreled questions. **Leading questions** are questions that consciously or unconsciously lead the respondent to a particular answer. For example, asking "We heard that attendance is a problem in your school. Is your child attending school?" could lead your respondent to answer the socially desirable rather than the accurate answer. Similarly, **double-barreled questions** are those that ask the respondent two different things in one question. One example is "why do some children perform well in their studies and why do some cause a lot of trouble?" This question is actually asking two different and separate things.[41]

In the previous paragraphs I have talked about the different ways to ask questions (and particular ways of avoiding certain survey instrument mistakes). However, the most important aspect of this is to ask yourself, **"Does the research instrument provide answers to your research question?"** If you go back to the example, the research is about how the parent's attitudes affect the child's performance. You will notice though that there were no questions about the parent's attitudes, aside from the question asking about schooling's importance. This is actually a very common mistake when one does the whole survey very well but the survey fails to answer the primary research question. Thus, you will have to be careful with how your research instrument connects to and helps answer your main question, or how it provides evidence for your research argument.

In this relatively longer section, I hope to have highlighted the importance of being careful and thorough when you are doing your research instrument, particularly your survey questionnaire. Being careful about this could save you a lot of time and trouble in the future especially since it is costly to repeat your survey once it does not give you the data needed for your research.

3.4 Interview and FGD mistakes

For qualitative social science and management research, the data will usually come less from surveys and more from observations, interviews, and focus group discussions (FGDs). **Interviews** are focused on individual participants while **FGDs** usually involve more than two invited participants with shared characteristics to discuss a particular topic related to the research question. One of the most common mistakes is to **mindlessly use** and conflate the two methods for research. A common mistake is when researchers do interviews and FGDs with the same people. For example, they interview farmers individually and then ask them again to come as a group to join a focus group discussion. On the other hand, there are others who thought it would be better to just have one FGD with 8-10 people rather than go through the trouble of having eight individual interviews. However, you must remember that FGDs are as much about the interaction as they are about the participants' answers.

You should know that there are particular reasons for **preferring one over the other**, and that you should be deliberate and discerning about which research method to use. Interviews often work best when you are researching on sensitive or confidential topics, individual narratives, professional expertise/ ideas, in-depth information, or personal opinions and perspectives. On the other hand, FGDs work best when you are researching on people's variety of perspectives, a community's information, a subpopulation's social norms, or a group's perception about a product.[42] Research on one's personal experience of grief and loss may be better suited to an interview just as research on women's cosmetic preference will be better understood with an FGD. To see if you should use one over the other, you have to know the **type of information** you plan to obtain from your respondent and how this **relates to the research question**. Of course, your research can use a mix of interviews and FGDs but you just have to be deliberate about which participants will best respond to individual interviews and which will best respond to FGDs.

Once you have settled the question of which one to use, you will have to invite your informants and schedule their interviews. Here again is an opportunity to commit a number of crucial mistakes, such as not giving enough information, not providing enough lead time, and not writing the invitation in a professional manner. First, you will have to give **enough information** to the people you will interview or whose constituents you will interview. Some researchers have approached parents in a school without informing the school principal, and this is a big mistake. If you ever plan to do a research, you should first ask permission from the institutional gatekeepers: principals, barangay captains, mayors, or entrepreneurs. Additionally, you will have to inform both the gatekeepers and the participants about the nature and purpose of your study, the time commitment, and how the information will be used. Section 3.7 will discuss more about the necessary information contained in your invitation letter to your research participants.

A second thing to consider is how much time you give your informants to **prepare** for your interview or FGD. Due to the personal nature of Filipinos, there have been instances when the invitation was sent—or the person was just informed about the interview—on the day of the actual interview. Here it is important to consider and be sensitive to the work and prior commitments your informants might have. As a rule of thumb, a week for them to respond to your invitation should be enough time. You may even want to just ask them casually first, and then only after, send a formal invitation to have an interview. If you know that a particular person is busy (for example, a president or chief executive of a company), it will be best to schedule more than a week in advance and provide them with options for the dates to have the interview.

A third mistake to consider is the **manner** in which you write your invitation. With the presence of Facebook and other forms of social media, some students just write a quick instant message to their friends if they can be interviewed. I argue, however, that research is a professional activity and should be treated as a means of introducing students into a more professional environment. Thus, you will have to learn some basics about e-mail etiquette. Some mistakes include:

- not writing a subject line on the e-mail,
- simply attaching a Word document and not saying what the letter is about,
- writing the wrong addressee,
- not clarifying when you want to hear from the respondents again, and
- using informal language.

To address these, remember to have a **short subject line** so that your interviewees will know what the invitation is about. A subject such as "Invitation to an Interview for [name of respondent]" should work fine. Second, even if your invitation is in an attached document (I suggest transforming the Word file into a PDF), your email body should not be blank. It will be best to inform your participant briefly **what is in the attachment**. Third, the space on the top left of your letter (just below the date) should be your informant's name, affiliation, and/or address. I have seen people write their own (researcher's) names on this section; please do not commit this mistake. Fourth, you will need to politely ask your informant when you wish to hear from them so that you know when to look for another informant. Lastly, you will have to be more mindful of your language. This is not a place where you just ask your respondent "Dear Ma'am, Can you be our interviewer? Thanks…" Again, research is a professional activity, and writing these invitations is a way to practice this professionalism ahead of working in a professional environment.

After scheduling the interview, you will have to prepare for it. Ideally, you should have an **interview guide**, script, or talking points. Preparing this document will help you focus your interview so that you are on track in answering your main research question. You will have to note that there are different ways of doing interviews, and you will have to again be intentional about your format.

Unstructured interviews are conversations where you ask your respondents about a topic without a predetermined structure, flow, or format; this works best if you are establishing rapport and getting to know more about the research. **Semi-structured interviews** are meetings where you are guided but do not have to strictly follow a set of questions; this is best when you want guidance and flexibility as you ask your respondents. **Structured interviews** are verbal questionnaires where the interaction is limited to your asking a fixed set of questions; this is best used when you want demographic details, standard answers, and uniform data.[43]

Although you will have to be deliberate about your choice, it is perfectly fine also that there are parts of the interviews more structured than others. For example, you may want to have a structured interview at the start when you obtain standard data on the person's "characteristics" like age, education, occupation, and so on. After getting these information, you may move to a semi-structured interview where you ask your participant about ideas, opinions, or perceptions about your research topic. As you glance at your interview guide, you can also ask questions that slightly deviate from your predetermined questions.

When you do an interview or FGD guide, be sure to have a **coherent yet flexible structure** to guide your thinking and your informant's answering. An incoherent interview guide shows that you did not make an effort to organize your thoughts prior to the interview; this may make your participant question your research credibility, and it could lead to time being wasted because you keep shuttling from one question to another. Inasmuch as it is important to be flexible, there is a need to learn how to structure your questions. Do you plan to start with broad ideas and go to specifics later? Or do you plan to ask specific concrete questions first and then move to the more abstract ones later? Will you divide the questions according to a logical progression in terms of time, or in terms of themes? And finally, how do your interview questions relate back to your main research question?

When doing interviews, a common mistake is to just stick to the script and bypass important insights that your informant is saying. It is so easy to aim to ask only those questions you prepared for. But when you do this, you limit yourself to confirming what you already have in your head rather than opening yourself to other people's answers. Thus, you will have to be sensitive to how new and exciting ideas can come from your respondents. Given this, you have to learn how to ask **follow-up questions** when these interesting ideas come up. If your interviewee says something surprising, how will you react? Will you just sweep it under the rug or will you ask your interviewee to say more about it? Since answers in the interviews will form the base of research, you will have to get rich and meaningful data, and these often come with your follow-up questions. Preparing for those follow-up questions will be a good exercise to help mine rich data.

3.5 Untranscribed and uncoded data

Now that you have your interview guide prepared and your interview scheduled, you will have to go on to the interview proper. Although this might seem like a no-brainer, there have been instances when researchers have **failed to record** an interview. Whether it is because they simply forgot to bring a voice recorder or because they thought they could write fast or memorize what their informants say, it is nonetheless a big mistake to rely solely on one's memory. After all, the human mind is prone to remembering only the things it wants to hear and remember. Thus, you must make it a point to bring a **recording device**; most smartphones are already equipped with this.

After doing the interviews, there is a strong temptation to just **store the recordings** on one's computer and just go back to it when necessary. However, professional qualitative researchers make it a point to **transcribe all interviews** so that data analysis will be much easier. This means that you have to listen to your interviews and type them up in a document. It sounds easy but it can eat up a lot of your time, so it will be good to prepare yourself. You might also think that since you don't need to use all of your interviews, you will just type those that will be useful. This, however, is a bad idea because there might be some quotes that are used out of context and will be meaningless.

Even if it will take some time, it is best that you transcribe most of what was recorded (you can forego transcribing the hi's and hello's at the start of your interview). To do your transcription, you need to write details at the start of when and where the interview happened, and then write the interviewer and interviewee's names. After this, you can type up your transcription in the same way you type a script. You should write the person speaking and what was said immediately after. For example:

> Jan: What is unique about Filipino dishes?
> Pete: Filipino dishes are rather flavorful and a mix of different cuisines....

Once you have these interviews transcribed, you do not just get quotes and use those quotes for your research. Rather, you should familiarize yourself with the data, re-read it, and search for themes that relate to your research. This is the part when you create a **code,** or a "word or short phrase that symbolically assigns a summative, salient, essence-capturing, and/or evocative attribute for a portion of language-based or visual data."[44] When you code qualitative research, you have to highlight a particular interview answer and tag it with a code that relates to what is known in the literature or one of the broader themes you are investigating. In the example above, you can code it as "mixed cuisine."

There are computer software that help with qualitative data analysis, but doing the highlighting and tagging can also be done in your usual word processor. You may even do it old-school by typing up your interview transcript, printing them on paper, highlighting certain quotes, and placing a code as a marginal note. By doing this **systematic coding**, you make sure that you are able to connect concrete answers from your interviewers to the more abstract concepts and themes from the literature. The transcribing and coding also guards against possible bias with just cherry-picking the quotes that connect with your hypothesis or tentative argument rather than what your data is actually showing.

3.6 Unaddressed ethical concerns

When your research involves working with human participants and publishing (that is, making public) your results, you will often be asked to obtain **research ethics approval** from an institutional review board or research ethics committee. Being unable to seek research ethics approval for your research is a costly mistake, especially when you have funding for your work or plan to publish your work in reputable journals. Most research funders require that your research should pass through ethics approval and most journals only accept papers that have been given ethics approval. This preoccupation with ethics is for funders and journals to know that an independent body has reviewed your methods and found them compliant with ethical standards. It must be noted that retrospective research ethics approval is often not permitted; this means that you cannot collect data and only then seek ethics approval for the data you *already* collected.[45]

But why this concern for research ethics? On the one hand, the research ethics approval protects the research respondents or participants, who should know about the **consequences** of their participation or non-participation in a research, clarify how they will be **compensated** (if at all), learn how their **confidentiality** will be protected, and be asked for their **informed consent**. There have been many cases when human research was advanced without any form of independent review, which has led to some abuses from otherwise upstanding scientists and researchers. During World War II, "medical experiments" were performed on Jews who did not consent to their participation in them. For example, there were experiments that immersed research participants in ice cold water and sought to answer which "treatment" worked best for hypothermia.[46] More recently, ethical concerns have come in subtler forms such as particular people not being given medication because of a medical trial, or qualitative researchers being insensitive in phrasing their questions.

On the other hand, it must also be noted that research ethics approval also **protects the researcher and institution**. For researchers, ethics approval helps them clarify their intention for the research project and the comments of the ethics board could actually help better the collection and analysis of data. Additionally, the approval of a research ethics committee also helps researchers so that they do not conduct research that may potentially damage their reputation. For institutions, assuring that their scientists and researchers are able to conduct ethical research helps deter them from engaging in ethically unacceptable behavior. This consequently helps institutions avoid legal action and unfavorable publicity that may come if these actions or research are committed.[47]

Although different institutions do ethical approval differently, a research ethics approval application usually takes more than two weeks to be reviewed, so you will have to take into consideration this time element. Additionally, writing the application and filling out the application form for ethics approval may again take time and effort. Thus, it may seem like an added burden to go through ethical approval. But if one is given the right perspective—treating the process as a necessary step to ensure ethical practice that helps research participants, researchers, and institutions—then, this will surely be a meaningful exercise.

Aside from filling out your research ethics application, you will also have to consider if you involve **vulnerable populations** in your research. This means that there are some people who are treated with greater care in research because they too are more likely and are prime candidates for exploitation. These include *prisoners* who have lost their civil liberties, *children* who are unable to give full consent, *incompetent adults* (those with some mental disability) who are unable to make autonomous decisions, or *disadvantaged people* who may be easily swayed by material gain or financial reward.[48] Although it is not impossible to do research with them, there will be unique circumstances that have to be considered. For example, for children, the consent letters should be addressed to parents who will give their consent but children will also have to be told about the nature of the study and should give their assent to joining the study. For prisoners, you will have to assure that they are not forced into participating in your research and that their identities are protected.

Aside from the inability to consider how some populations are vulnerable and need more care when one does research, there is also the mistake of being **unable to protect the privacy and confidentiality** of the research respondent. Privacy means that part of a person's life that is not governed by society's laws—that is, one's private life. Confidentiality means the ethical nondisclosure expected when one is provided information and should prevent anyone from accessing this information.[49] When doing research, there are times when privacy is violated but confidentiality is maintained. For example, your respondent says that he has another family; the person's privacy has been violated. But if your respondent asks you not to tell this to anyone and you maintain it, you are honoring the confidentiality.

To protect the privacy of your respondent, there may be times when the use of **aliases** or **pseudonyms** is preferred. In general, it is best practice to use these aliases when reporting your research—particularly when your research goes into sensitive topics or have negative consequences when people's identities are revealed. For example, a mechanic may lose his job if he talks about the unfair labor practices in a company, and his name gets disclosed in a research. Additionally, providing a lot of details about the mechanic (or his company) may lead to the person's being eventually found. Thus, there are some research that tell you at the start of the research that certain details have been changed in order to protect the identities of individuals and communities. These changes in details, however, should be said at the start of your research and should not interfere with the arguments and conclusions of your research. For public officials and experts, it is usually the case that their details are known and so you will have to ask them if it will be alright for them to be named and acknowledged in your research.

To **maintain confidentiality** of the participant, it will be best for you to ask at the end of the interview if there are particular information revealed that the respondent does not want to be included in the research report. You will also have to ensure how the data will be stored properly so that access to the information will be limited to those who are written in the research ethics application. It is important for the participant to know the people who will have access to his or her information, and how the information will be used. To honor the informant's confidentiality, you will have to disclose how your data will be stored and who can access these data.

These pieces of information are usually in the form of quotations from interviews or answers from survey respondents, and these would generally have to be anonymized, that is, readers should not be able to trace who wrote or spoke about something written in the research output. However, there are other types of research methods and practices that involve participants being photographed or video-recorded. In these cases, a separate **photo and video release form** should be created so that participants will know when and how their photos will be used. If your participants' photographs will be included in your final research output, you will have to inform them and get their consent. They should say that they are willing for their photographs to be used publicly, and you will have to honor their request if they desire that these not be used in public (e.g. in books, photo exhibits, website).

Another ethical concern that not a lot of researchers think about is when researchers think of their informants as mere sources of information, and merely "use" them as a means of obtaining information. Although there is the importance of objectivity in research, having human participants means that we are working with creatures who have emotions, are social, and have their dignity. If we go into a community and want only to get information from them, it is as if we are saying that once we get information, we can be out of that community. In a sense when we do research, we have a responsibility to the people we work with, and we have to treat these respondents not merely as sources of information but also as people who have something to teach us.

3.7 Inability to foresee and disclose risks

Every day, there are some risks people are exposed to. A dysfunctional chair has the potential of injuring a person; an unscrupulous chef may serve a dish that can cause food poisoning; a person crossing the street may meet an accident; a person, without meaning to, may say something offensive and thus make another person feel unsafe. All of these are risks that people experience in daily life. However, since research will involve intentionality, people may be exposed to risks that could be greater than those experienced in daily life.

When working on a research, you, too, will have to think about and ask what risks are present for your research participants. This is most salient for medical research when drug tests involve certain groups getting a treatment and other groups getting a *placebo*, or a fake treatment to see if the real treatment works.[50] There are risks of harmful side effects, of the placebo group having worse outcomes, of the treatment group becoming unhealthier if the treatment stops, and other risks that come along with it. Since the typical reader of this book may not be doing medical research soon, you may think that you are exempted from this task of **foreseeing the risks** of your research. However, you still have to assess the likelihood and severity of the possible risks. Here are some examples of them:

- **Physical risks-** When your research involves the movement of someone (e.g. testing the physical strength of athletes), you should think about the physical risks involved. Are participants likely to be injured? Will they likely experience exhaustion? How likely will they be harmed by something you ask them to do? You have to ask these questions as you conceptualize your research.
- **Psychological risks-** When doing interviews or surveys, there are times when you will have to ask sensitive questions of your participants. You may have questions on their family background, sexual orientation, or personal histories, and these questions may elicit negative psychological feelings of regret, disappointment, sadness, anger, or trauma. In these cases, you will have to clarify how your questions might actually elicit emotions from your participants. Additionally, sometimes your research is itself a sensitive topic (e.g. family trauma, personal tragedy, school pressures). During these times, you will have to think thoroughly about the potential risks for your participants and maybe even for yourself.
- **Social risks-** When someone discloses an unacceptable social behavior in a focus group discussion, there is the risk of

this person being judged or ostracized. When your research exposes the illicit family of a person, both legal and illicit families may suffer the negative consequences. Although these can be extreme cases, it emphasizes how social risks are present when you do research. Thus, you will have to clarify how your research contributes to negative social effects for your research participants.

- **Legal risks-** When your research exposes someone for a crime, this can lead to legal risks of criminal charges being given. If your research on illegal drugs exposes the magnitude of a community's participation, this may have legal and extra-legal consequences. If your research highlights a person's ill feelings for a company's labor practice, the company may seek legal remedies since their name has been tarnished. Thus, you will have to also foresee how your research can lead to legal risks and action for your respondents and yourself.

Of course, it is about not just foreseeing the risks but also *disclosing* them, *minimizing* their likelihood, and *having a plan* if the negative incidents happen. In your consent form, you should tell your participants the possible risks for their involvement. Although the risks are unlikely to happen, your **disclosing the risks** shows that you are prepared to address them if they do ever happen. Telling your respondents about the risks also tells them that you have thought deeply about your research.

Aside from foreseeing and disclosing these risks, you will also have to learn how to **minimize the risks**. If you see that there are physical risks, you have to know what objects or activities could help reduce the risk (e.g. stretching, floor mats, proper attire). If you know that there are psychological risks, you may want to try to find other ways of creatively asking a question or of preparing your respondent for a sensitive topic. If you foresee a social or legal risk, you can find ways to keep the confidentiality of the other person. These are just some ways of minimizing risks, and you will have to find other ways if you foresee risks unique to your research.

Lastly, you will have to come **prepared with a plan** should the negative event happens. If you know that there is a risk of injury, it will be a wise idea to have a first aid kit available and have someone who has undergone first aid training. Additionally, it will be good to know the location and hotline for the nearest hospital or clinic. If you know that there is risk of psychological discomfort, it may be a good idea to have the phone number of a nearby psychologist or psychological center. If there are social or legal risks, you may want to consult with a lawyer or a more experienced researcher on what options you have. Again, it is much better that you have these things planned ahead even if it does not happen than to panic and scramble if it does.

Although the risks are often thought about in terms of the risks for your participants, you will also have to think about the **risks to yourself**. Is it possible that you will also experience physical, psychological, social, or legal risks when you do your research? Are these risks more than those typically experienced in daily life? What can you do to minimize risks to yourself and what is your plan if a negative incident happens?

3.8 Inability to obtain informed consent

When doing research with human participants, you will have to get clear consent from them, and one common mistake is to **not document the consent** that was given. Although a person may implicitly consent to an interview, the lack of documentation could be bad for both the research participant and the researcher. For research participants, having no documentation means that they do not have a written document that details the procedure, risks, benefits, and goal of the study. It is important for them to have these details so that they know exactly what is being asked of them. For researchers, having no documentation means that you do not have proof that the person indeed consented to your research. People may actually sue you and say their consent was not obtained, and you have no defense because you did not document your participants' consent.

Thus, you will have to find a way to document your research participants' consent. The most common form this takes is through an **informed consent form**, where you detail the goals, procedures, risks, benefits, and so on of your research project. The form, which can come as an invitation, should provide the details at the start, then end with a place for people to affix their signature of concurrence. It is like a contract that details the terms at the start and asks parties to sign at the end. Here are some important details that you will have to include in your consent form:

- **Purpose of the study:** You will have to tell your respondent what is the study for (e.g. class project, graduate thesis, or research publication), who is funding the project, and what are the broad research questions that you want answered or the broad objectives of your research project.
- **Procedure and duration of involvement:** After showing the purpose, you will have to detail the procedure and what you are requesting from your participant. Will the participant be a survey respondent, an interviewee, or a person in a focus group discussion? What are the possible questions that will be asked? How much time will be needed for the participation? The detail about the average time it will take to finish is particularly important since your respondent needs to know if he or she has time.
- **Potential risks and benefits**: As a way of helping participants think more rationally about their participation, you will have to clarify the pros and cons of joining the study. Will joining the study benefit their knowledge of themselves? Will it benefit systems, processes, or policies? Will there be risks involved? It is best to clarify these at the start, and even detail how risks will be minimized and how the benefits outweigh the risks. Please do not include monetary compensation as a potential benefit from your study since you would not want your participant to be unduly influenced by this benefit.
- **Statement of voluntary participation and right to withdraw**: You will have to write that the person may choose not to participate in the study and may withdraw from the study anytime without any negative consequence for the research participant. You will also have to say that the participant may choose not to answer questions that one is not comfortable with, and that data can be withdrawn even after the interview or survey.
- **Ensure confidentiality of data:** You will have to write how

you will protect the privacy of the individual. You may say that the data will be anonymous, and that they cannot be traced back to the information. If you need to write the names of your respondents (e.g. for public figures and experts), you may say that you are requesting for their names to be mentioned but that you will respect their decision not to disclose their names in the final report. You may also write who are the people who have access to the data, and how their data are protected.

- **Permission for recording:** You will have to tell your reader if you are requesting for the interview or focus group discussion to be audio- or video-recorded for your research. If you plan to do recording, who are the people who have access to this? Will the recording be heard or shown in public? It will be good to also detail why there is the need for the recording in the first place; often, it is about capturing faithfully what were said by the research participants.
- **Compensation**: Another detail you will have to write is the compensation (or the lack of compensation) for the time your informant spent on your research. Compensation can come in the form of a modest honorarium, a travel allowance, some food or meal, a small token, or a chance to be included in a lottery. You may also say that there is no compensation for participation in the study.
- **Contact numbers:** It is often best practice to write the contact details of yourself, your adviser, or your institutional research ethics office, so that questions or concerns may be addressed through the right channels.

These are just the **minimum facts** that should be detailed in your informed consent forms. If there are additional details that you feel your research participants should know, you should definitely include them in your consent forms. At the end of your consent forms, you should have tick boxes that detail the person's consent to your research:

☐ I agree to participate in this study…
☐ I do not wish to participate in this study…

☐ I allow my real name to be used…
☐ I do not allow my real name to be used…

☐ I allow the audio/video-recording of my responses…
☐ I do not allow the audio/video-recording of my responses… But the researchers may write down by hand, or type, my answers.

At the end of the consent form, you should ask your research participant to write their name in print, sign above, and write the date it was signed. Although the details written here are in English, you will have to consider the language your respondents are most comfortable in. You will likely have to create a translation if you plan to work with a local language. Additionally, in some places with low literacy (people are unable to read and write fully), you will likely have to explain or read aloud the consent form.

3.9 Unclear methods discussion

At this point, you may have done all the planning and all the executing for you to collect your data through surveys, interviews, focus group discussions, or observations. It will be tempting to analyze your data already and **forget writing** how you collected them. However, it will be your task as researcher to let your readers know the process you went through with collecting your data. You have to clarify what were the steps you took for you to arrive at your results and not just talk about the research method you used.

For both qualitative and quantitative research, you should discuss your **participants,** how they were recruited, what they were asked to do or answer, how many they were, and what were unique about them. You will need to detail the justification for choosing your participants, the means you used to invite them, and your sampling procedure (Is it random sampling or snowball sampling?). For quantitative research and qualitative research with a big sample, you can add the **characteristics of the sample**: the age range of the respondents, their gender composition, their similarities or differences with each other. For qualitative research with a small sample size, you can add the names/pseudonyms and characteristics of your individual interviewees. You can detail a short biography about those who were interviewed in-depth, particularly if these details are important for your study.

Aside from having details about the participants, you should also write the **data collection mechanism** and the **research instruments**. You may detail how you gave a survey or how you got data from an open source data bank. You may also say something about the interviews, and how these were conducted. Additionally, it will be good to say what were the broad questions that were asked either in the survey or in the interviews, and how these relate to your main research question.

For quantitative research, you will have to detail the **variables** that are important for your research. Sometimes the variables can just be listed, particularly if you are just interested in population increase, personal preferences, etc. However, there will be times when you have to detail which are the *dependent*, *independent*, and *control* variables. In statistics, this is particularly important for **inferential statistics** when you try to approximate how particular factors (variables) influence or affect an outcome.

Take, for example, a study that tries to ask if one's educational attainment affects the salary of the individual. The intuition is that an individual who has more years of education (who has a higher educational attainment) is more likely to have a higher salary. The variable the researcher is interested to explain is often called the **dependent variable**; this is the outcome or effect that one wants to study. In the example, *salary* is the dependent variable because this is the one we are interested to explain. Similarly, the variable that could likely explain the outcome is what is called the **independent variable**; this is also called the explanatory variable. In the example, we hypothesize that *educational attainment* could explain the differences in people's salaries, so this is our main independent variable.[51]

However, we also know that the salary of an individual is also affected by other factors like gender, prior socioeconomic status, and the industry one works in. There have been studies that suggest that males earn relatively higher than female, that those who have higher socioeconomic status are more likely to earn more, and that those who work in the technology and business sectors earn more than those in other industries.[52] In this case, we want to account for these added factors, which are called **control variables**, or the variables that are kept constant or the same, so that they do not "mix" with the main independent variable. In this example, these other "factors" should be kept constant so that we know the true effect of the main independent variable, which is educational attainment.

When writing a research, you will have to clearly identify and accurately describe your dependent, independent, and control variables. You should also show how the variables are appropriate in approximating the answer for your research question.

Aside from the variables, you have to show how you did your **data analysis**. You may have **descriptive statistics** that detail the measures of central tendency and variability, or the percentage of a particular group. For example, you can write about the mean and standard deviation of salary and educational attainment (in number of years). You may also write the percentage in your sample who are male or female, who work in business, manufacturing, academe, etc., or who come from urban or rural areas. In this way, you show the composition of your sample.

You may also detail how you will **visualize** your results, using *pie charts* to show the distribution in a sample, or *bar graphs* for the number of people who belong in a particular category. One can also use a *time plot* that shows how a variable has changed through time, or a *scatter plot* that shows the interaction between two variables (e.g. educational attainment and salary). In this sense, you will have to detail in your methods section data visualization techniques you will use.

Tabular data may also be done, as with cross-tabulations that show how groups have different means, standard deviations, or percentages. For example, males and females may have different numbers of years of education, or salaries. This can be shown in a table, and

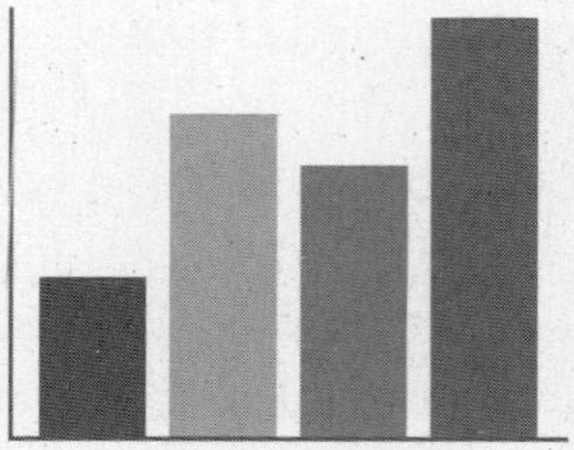

Bar Graph

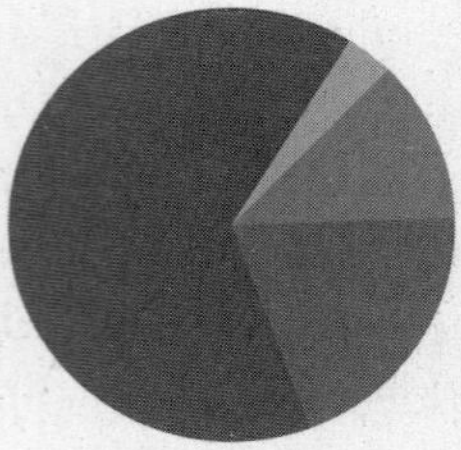

Pie Chart

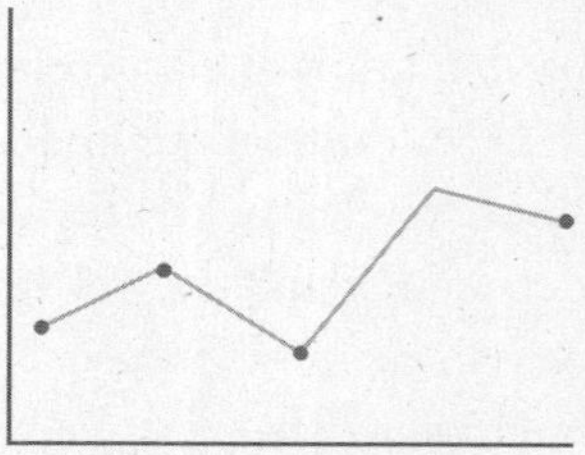

Time Plot

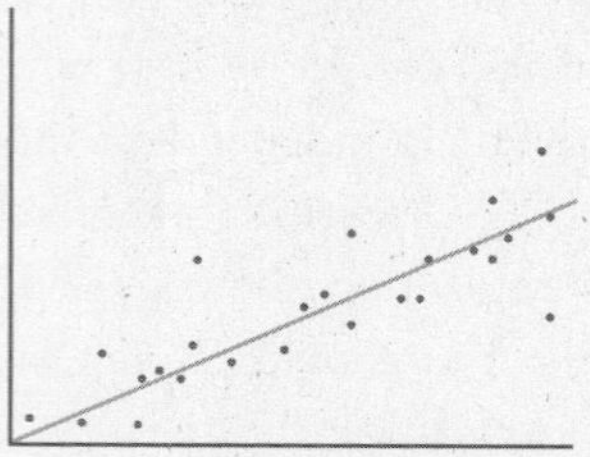

Scatter Plot

if you are interested in showing if these differences are statistically significant, you will have to do an **analysis of variance**. This is usually done with hypothesis testing, where at least two means or percentages are compared to see if the differences between them are statistically significant. For example, you are interested to know if males and females have different monthly salaries on average. To do this, you will have to do hypothesis testing where your research hypothesis is that the average salary for males is different from the average salary for females. Average is denoted by the Greek letter mu (μ):

$$H_1: \mu_{male} \neq \mu_{female}$$

Consequently, the null hypothesis is that the average salary of males is similar to the average salary of females.

$$H_0: \mu_{male} = \mu_{female}$$

To prove that the average monthly salaries of males and females are **statistically significantly different** from each other, the two means have to be compared. To ascertain they are different, the probability of the null hypothesis, H_0, should be less than 0.05. This means that the probability that both means are equal is very unlikely—that the likelihood of equal means is less than 5 in 100. In your methods section, you will have to show that you will be doing these tabulations and analyses of variance.

Two other ways of doing basic statistical analyses are through correlations and regressions. **Correlations** highlight the strength of the relationship between two variables being studied. Correlations are numbers (technically they are termed *coefficients*) from -1 to 1, with 0 meaning no correlation. A positive coefficient close to one means that there is a **positive correlation**, where an increase in one variable means an increase in another variable. For example, a higher score in math may be correlated with a higher score in science since both utilize logic and careful analysis. This is a positive correlation. However, a higher score in math can hypothetically be related with a lower score in physical education. This does not mean that the correlation is zero; rather it is negative. A negative coefficient close to negative one means that there is **negative correlation,** where one variable increases as the other decreases. If two variables are not related, the coefficient is closer to zero (whether positive or negative) and this means there is no correlation.[53]

In your research, you can show the relationship between the different variables and see which ones have strong correlations. Although there are debates on what is considered a strong correlation, it is usually assumed that coefficients of 0.3 to 0.6 are substantial while above 0.6 are strong.[54] Showing these correlations can help show which variables are influencing the dependent variable or which variables influence each other.

Regressions provide the effect or influence of the independent variables on the dependent variable. Similar to correlations, they too have coefficients, and these coefficients mean the change in the dependent variable for every one unit increase in the independent variable. For example, a study looks at how the number of years of education affects one's salary. In this case, the number of years of education is the **independent variable** while the person's salary is the **dependent variable**. After doing a simple linear regression on a data analysis software, the coefficient may turn out to be PHP 1,300. This means that a one-year increase in education is related to a PHP 1,300 increase in one's salary.

However, we do not just look at the **regression coefficient** since we also have to see the ***p-value***, or the probability that your coefficient supports the null hypothesis. The *p-value* is a number from 0 to 1, often interpreted in this way:

- A small *p-value* (less than 0.05) indicates strong evidence against the null hypothesis, which means that you have reason to believe that your coefficient is significant.
- A large *p-value* (more than 0.05) indicates weak evidence against the null hypothesis, which means that you fail to reject the null hypothesis.
- A *p-value* close to the cut-off (0.05) is marginal and could be either statistically significant or insignificant.[55]

In studies that involve regressions, the *p-value* is usually denoted by asterisks, where one asterisk means a *p-value* of less than 0.05, two asterisks mean a value of less than 0.01, and three asterisks mean a value of less than 0.001. In statistical tables, these are usually shown at the bottom with this notation: $^{*}p < 0.05$, $^{**}p < 0.01$, $^{***}p < 0.001$. What this means is that the **more asterisks** you have, the **higher the statistical significance** and the more reasons you have for believing in the influence of the independent variable on the dependent variable. In the example earlier of PHP 1300 increase in salary for every one year addition in education, if the coefficient's level of significance is below 0.001, it means that there is strong evidence to suggest that education is a variable that influences people's salaries.

For qualitative research, you will have to talk about the various questions you asked from your respondents and how these questions are related to your research argument or the themes you are pursuing. If you are using an **interview guide** or a **questionnaire**, it will be good to write about this briefly in the body of the methods section and refer your reader to an appendix for the full research instrument. For qualitative data analysis, you will have to inform your readers about how you **transcribed**, **coded**, and **searched for themes** in your research. You will have to show that you did systematic study rather than simply picking quotes that you find useful.

The common mistake in the methods section of a research happens when researchers do not give enough details about how data was collected and analyzed. In this sense, it is better to err on the side of giving a lot of details rather than having no details at all. By telling people about the details of your data collection and analysis, you become transparent about your process, and your readers are more likely to understand how you arrive at your conclusions.

3.10 Difficult-to-find resources

In the previous sections, the concentration is on obtaining data from human participants and natural events (whether in the social or natural sciences). However, there are also research studies that concentrate on using **archived and historical materials**, like old newspapers, books, letters, photographs, manuscripts, and so on. The difficulty with using these types of materials is the access you can have since these materials are usually placed in institutional archives or family *bodegas*. One mistake is to not foresee how this inaccessibility can pose a problem for your research.

When working with archived materials, it will be best to strategize how you will obtain access for these materials. If you plan to research on Jose Rizal's letters and other documents, you may first want to ask for advice from experts who have studied Rizal, such as Professor Ambeth Ocampo. A second place to consider would be the National Archives and the National Library, which have a good number of these documents or could at least point you to other sources of Rizaliana materials. It will also be good to know the policies of the libraries and archives you visit. Requirements may include:

- Student or teacher ID card;
- Fees to be paid upon entering the premises or photocopying;
- Formal referral letter from the librarian of your school;

- Formal letter detailing the project and needed materials from the archive; or
- Online appointments and reservations.

When you are able to access these places, you will have to know how to find your materials. There may be some materials that can be searched using the online catalog while there are some that can only be searched through a list of records and categories. It is best to have the general direction or research question so that you will know what to focus on when looking through and looking for sources.

Although archival and historical research will usually not involve human interaction, this does not mean that it is an easier endeavor. If anything, this type of research is actually a little more difficult than the typical social or natural science research because the whole research depends on the **availability of resources**. In the context of the Philippines, where written and tangible materials are not often well preserved, the dearth and unreliability of sources could pose a real problem. Additionally, there are times when Philippine materials are not found in the Philippines but in archives in foreign countries, like the United States Library of Congress, the British Museum, or the Archivo Histórico Nacional in Spain. Unless you have deep pockets—and even if you have deep pockets—the financial investment to go to these archives will likely be a deterrent.

The lesson here is to anticipate the **possible challenges** that can come along when working with archived documents. This challenging work provides its own contribution to scholarship and knowledge, and it is important to be prepared for the challenges rather than be caught off-guard when they arise.

CHAPTER 4
MISTAKES IN PRESENTATION AND ANALYSIS

Once you have gathered your data, you will have to present them in your results section, and interpret them in your discussion section. In scientific journals, the results and discussion sections are usually separate so that the reader may know which data are from the experiments, interviews, surveys and firsthand information of the researcher, and which data are the interpretation of these firsthand information and its interaction with secondary data. There are times, however, when they are combined to enhance readability.[56]

In quantitative studies' results section, you will have to present **tables** and/or **graphs**, and have to explain what these mean. In qualitative studies, you will have to write **quotations** and/or **observations**, and organize these according to the ideas you wish to pursue in your research. In either case, you will have to interpret the results in a **discussion section** that tries to *make sense* of the numbers or quotes you have. In the discussion section, you will also have to include previous research discoveries and how your research furthers what we already know about a topic.

Since writing the results and discussion section will seem highly technical, a beginning researcher without much exposure to scientific writing may find it difficult to write these sections, and consequently, make a lot of mistakes. In this chapter, common mistakes are discussed so that they can be avoided or prevented. For quantitative research these mistakes could include incorrect figures and tables while for qualitative research these could include quotations out of nowhere or non-embodied participants. Of course, there are more serious mistakes like falsification of data and plagiarism, which if committed could have serious consequences for students, researchers, and academics. Thus, this chapter helps to dispel certain misconceptions and help you avoid these mistakes.

4.1 Fabricated and inaccurate data

One of the most prized "possessions" of a researcher is one's integrity, that is, one's moral uprightness and honesty in showing results. This is particularly important since readers will have to take your word that something happened, and that you are not making stuff up. Although your reputation as a scholar will be enhanced by the diversity of publications and highly cited papers, this reputation can easily go down the drain if you commit something that threatens your own **academic integrity**. There are many forms of academic misconduct but in this section, I focus on fabricated and inaccurate data. Later in this chapter, I will talk about plagiarism. Take a look at some of these examples:

> (1) After collecting data for your quantitative research, you obtained data from 57 respondents. However, you remember your teacher asking you to have at least 60 respondents. Since the deadline is fast approaching, you tell yourself that it is alright to just "answer the survey" for three other respondents. You inputted data, thinking about how three additional hypothetical participants would answer your survey questions. After doing this, you proceed with your data analysis and show the results.
>
> (2) After obtaining qualitative data, you will have to show how the interview answers map out to your main research question. At some point, you find out that you were unable to get information about a topic and it will be cumbersome for you to reach out to your respondents to ask another set of questions. Besides, you think that you know your respondent enough to actually presume how the person will answer your questions. Thus, you tried to create a quote that seems to sound like one of your interviewees but this interview only happened in your head.

In both examples, it was very easy to rationalize why you needed to make up data, and that such new data is not a big deal. After all, it was not as if you made up the whole study. You still did surveys and interviews, and you just merely added some information, which you were unable to get. Thus, you can easily justify why you did it.

Wrong! However subtle one's "additional information" may be, it is still a practice of **fabrication of data**. This means that you created false information—whether just some bits of information or the whole study altogether. Such fabrication is **academic dishonesty** and this misconduct is a grave offense against the research community. The previous mistakes on incoherent literature review and unclear data collection methods are mistakes that can be rectified but academic dishonesty threatens the very core of the researcher's integrity. Thus, this should not be taken lightly.

Other forms of fabrication may include inputting numbers when there are none at all, changing the statistical significance of results, writing observations that did not happen, exaggerating particular incidences, selectively submitting results that are convenient or relate to your main argument, and hiding results that challenge your research argument.[57] There can also be fabrication in terms of **citations**, where you include references in order to add to your list, possibly because there is a minimum number required. This citation fabrication may mean including publications that you did not read, that are unrelated but pad your bibliography, or that you created with fake titles and authors.

One of the more disturbing cases would be researchers having **lab reports** before the experiment was conducted—or even if the experiment was never conducted at all. In this sense, they already have a presumed result and they just try to put in different variations to these results. Research that uses quantitative methods is especially susceptible to these fabricated data because it is very easy to input numbers without other people noticing.

Although not as grave as premeditated fabrication, **inaccurate information** is also a common mistake that one should avoid. These may come in the form of wrong affiliation of your interviewee, or a mistake in the institution you are studying, or a detail that you were unable to disclose. During these times, you have to **verify the information** you get and err on the side of being more transparent. It will take time to verify different information but this is an important step to fostering the discipline of research.

When you fabricate your data, it will be difficult for people to really know and find out. After all, these are numbers or interviews that you say you have. With the pressure to publish significant and novel results, the temptation of fabricating data is actually quite high with very low consequences if one is not caught. However, true scholars know that their academic integrity is on the line during these scenarios, and one's integrity hopefully weighs much more than the possibility of a new publication.

4.2 Incorrect figures

When you present data for your quantitative research, it will usually be in the form of tables or figures, which include graphs, time/scatter plots, and charts. Some mistakes researchers make are having no figures at all, using the wrong figures, or forgetting to put certain details in the figures. But when is it advisable to have a figure rather than just write the numbers on the text? It is best to have a figure when (1) you want to show **trends** or **patterns** with your data, (2) you have to **summarize your data** quickly, and (3) when you need a visual explanation for a **sequence of events**.[58] Additionally, figures help provide a snapshot of your argument without the use of so many words. In section 4.4, I talk about the mistakes that come when your figures/tables do not connect (or are only repeated) with the body.

But how do you know which figure to use? Here, it will be helpful to familiarize yourself with the different figures that are at your disposal, and how they are often used.

- **Bar graphs** are often used when you want to know the frequency of respondents in a given category. For example, as a market researcher, you are interested to know how many cappuccinos were sold per month from January until June. On the vertical axis (called *y-axis*), you should write the frequency—that is,

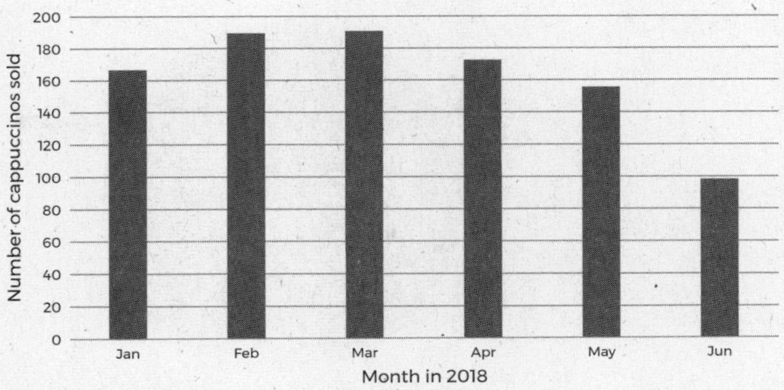

Figure 1. Cappuccinos sold per month

the number of cappuccinos sold. On the horizontal axis (called *x-axis*), you will need to write the category—for this example, the month.

- **Histograms** look similar to bar graphs, but instead of representing categories, the bars represent the frequency falling within a given range of numbers. In Figure 2, the *y-axis* shows the frequency of people while the *x-axis* shows the particular salary range. If you are interested to know the distribution of income, you will see that more people are earning between PHP 22,000 and 34,000 and that fewer people are earning above PHP 100,000.

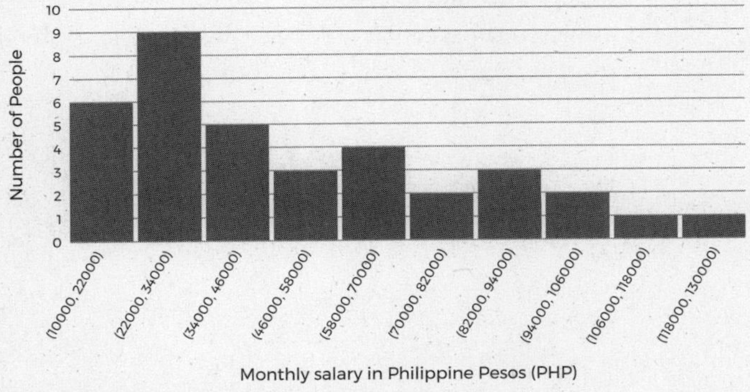

Figure 2. Monthly salary distribution

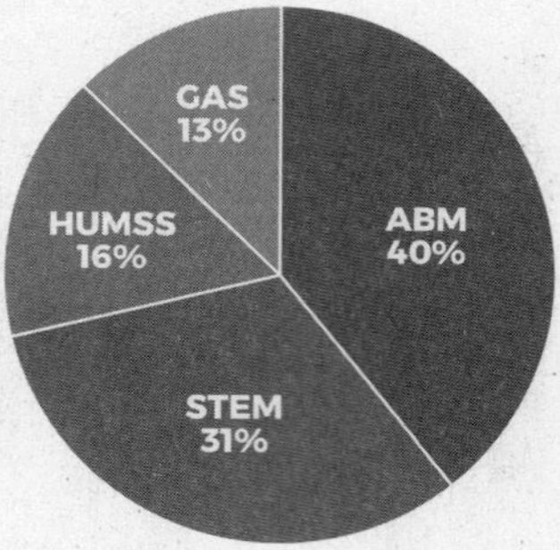

Figure 3. Senior High School Students Per Strand

- **Pie charts** are circular statistical graphs divided into slices that show the proportion occupied by particular groups or categories. In Figure 3, we see the ratio of senior high school students to the four academic strands. For example, 40% of the sample are from Accounting and Business Management while only 13% are in the General Academic Strand.
- A **line graph** is a display that shows information connected in some way. One type of line graph is the **time plot,** which is a graph where values are displayed against time. The *x-axis* is occupied by time, while the *y-axis* is for variables such as height, weight, population, number of students, etc. In Figure 4, the graph shows the number of published books or journals on the *y-axis* and the year of publication on the *x-axis*. The dots denote a particular number while the lines show the trend across the years.

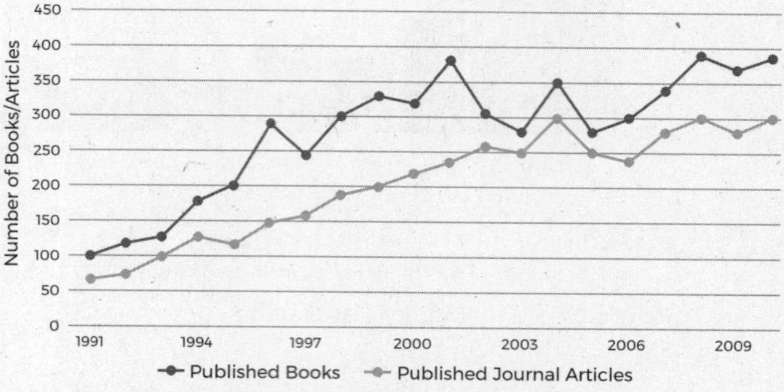

Figure 4. Books and Journal Articles Published Every Year

Hopefully, the discussion clarifies which type of graph is best to represent your data and argumentation accurately. After all, when working with ways of representing data, you will have to be deliberate and purposive in your choice of figure. The four graphs discussed are the most common ones but there are other types of graphs that you can use for your research. These include **scatter plots, box and whiskers graphs (box plots),** and **stemplots.**

Aside from using the wrong graph, there are other mistakes that come with the use of figures, graphs, and charts:

- **Figures without titles and captions**: It is important to remember that your figure should always be numbered (e.g. Figure 1) and have an appropriate title that captures succinctly what is shown in the graph (e.g. Cappuccinos served per month). If necessary, write a caption at the bottom that describes how the image may be read.
- **Figures without the correct labels**: For graphs that have *x* and *y-axes,* you have to label these axes correctly, telling your reader what the numbers on the vertical axis mean and what the categories on the horizontal axis signify. For pie charts, you will have to label the significant slices of the circular graph, and even write its proportion. Either way, you have to write labels and legends to help guide your reader.
- **Figures without clear source**: If your figure comes from someone else, you should write below the image the source of your figure.
- **Figures without focus**: If you want your readers to focus on something in your figure but fail to highlight it, you are making it more difficult for your reader to understand your main argument. If you want your reader to focus on a particular category, you may want to change the color of the bar to separate it from the other categories.
- **Scales that are not consistent**: If the first number on your *y-axis* is 0 and the second number is 5, and the third becomes 7, then the scales are no longer consistent. Thus, you will have to provide scales or intervals that are intuitive for your research (e.g. 0, 5, 10, 15… 0, 100, 200, 300…).

When working with figures, the most common mistake is to not assume the readers' perspective. Since you have done the research, you have an intuitive understanding of the results. However, your reader will need more information to help make sense of your information. The mistakes mentioned here often talk about the difficulty readers will have if you do not take them into consideration as you do your graphs.

4.3 Incorrect tables

Aside from mistakes in figures, researchers can also make mistakes when showing data in **tabular form.** One of the reasons you want to show data in tables is for your reader to immediately see both the trend and the details in your results. However, if your reader finds it hard to sift through your table and its details, you will have to find ways to improve the presentation of your tables. Here is one example of a table that may make your reader confused:

	Male	Female
Average Math test score	70.88	72.56
Average English test score	83.56	83.00
Median Age	16	16
Percentage Suspended	14.05	9.03

So what is wrong with the table above? For starters, you may have noticed that the table does not have a title, and so you do not know what to focus on. You may be asking yourself what the study is about and why there is the comparison between males and females. Second, you may wonder what the justifications are for the variables on the leftmost column. Third, you may be looking for the researcher's source of information. Fourth, the table itself is not very visually appealing and the presence of both vertical and horizontal lines seems to add more weight to an already dense table.

In this section, I discuss how these mistakes can be avoided by showing examples of **good tables** and outlining the **principles** behind the different examples. We provide tables for descriptive statistics, frequencies, correlations, and regressions. It is important

Table 1. Descriptive Statistics, n = 1406 students

	Mean	SD	Min	Max
Math test score	70.22	8.91	40	92
Reading test score	65.33	4.58	58	81
Age	9.12	0.32	8	11
Absence per month	2.41	0.66	0	5
Demographics				
Percentage Female	52.35	(736)		
Percentage Non-readers	11.31	(159)		
Percentage under CCT	24.39	(343)		

Source: Education Survey of 2018

Notes: The table shows descriptive statistics for the means and percentages of the variables of the 1406 students in the sample. Number in parenthesis shows the frequency.

to note that not all data need to be presented in tables since some data may have to be presented in figures while some do not need to be shown at all. You should distinguish your tables from your figures, and so, you should also number them separately and consecutively. In this section we will focus on the tables themselves while in the next section we will talk about the principles for analyzing tables and figures in prose form.

A **descriptive statistics table** is a table that provides the means and the standard deviations for the continuous variables, and the frequency or percentage for the categorical variables. **Continuous variables** are variables that have an infinite number of possible values, like height or weight. Since these variables provide us numbers, we can get the average number (*mean*) and the dispersion of the values from each other (*standard deviation*). Aside from the mean and standard deviation, one may also write the *range*, or the *minimum* and *maximum* values. On the other hand, **categorical variables** are variables that can be measured using a limited number of values or categories, like school placement or gender. Since these are categories, you will need to describe how many people belong to a group (*frequency*) or the proportion of a specific category's members in relation to the whole sample (*percentage*).[59]

Table 2. Frequency Table on Research Competency, n = 1406 students

	Strongly Disagree	Disagree	Neutral	Agree	Strongly Agree
I can do research.	67	79	430	623	207
I enjoy doing research.	132	273	317	521	163
I write good research papers.	141	332	267	444	222
I enjoy writing research papers.	239	369	460	210	128

Source: Education Survey of 2018

Notes: The table shows the number of people who agree or disagree with a given statement in the Likert scale survey.

Table 1 shows how descriptive statistics can be done for continuous and categorical variables. Some things to note are: (1) The table has a title that provides a snapshot of its contents and says the number of people who were included in the sample. (2) It clearly labels the mean, standard deviation, and extreme values for the continuous variables. From the example, we can see that math test scores are higher than reading test scores, and that the former is also more *dispersed* than the latter. When discussing this, you can talk about what could be factors affecting the higher scores and variability. (3) For the categorical variables, the table shows the percentage of people belonging to a group (e.g. female, those who are non-readers, and those who are under the government's conditional cash transfer program), and the frequency written within parentheses. (4) The bottom of the table shows the source of the information and the note that can guide the reader. (5) It will also be noted that rather than have vertical and horizontal lines cutting across all columns and rows, this table only has horizontal lines that are strategically placed at certain sections. If you view journal articles, most of them would have similar-looking tables.

Aside from descriptive statistics tables, there are other formats of tables you can use for your research. One such is a **frequency table** that shows how many of your respondents agree or disagree with a particular statement. Table 2 shows the number of people who agree

Table 3. Correlations Table, n = 1406 students

	1	2	3	4
1 Math test score	1.00			
2 Reading test score	0.88	1.00		
3 Age	0.12	0.08	1.00	
4 Absence per month	-0.53	-0.66	0.02	1.00

Source: Education Survey of 2018

Notes: The table shows correlations coefficients among different variables.

or disagree on a 5-point Likert scale. In this table, the title describes that it is about people's understanding of their research competency. It is important to also note that it is a frequency table. If you wish to show the *percentage* of the sample agreeing with a statement, you may write that it is a **percentage table**. You must also make sure that the total of the values for every horizontal line is equal to the number of people in your sample, or equal to 100 percent if you are using a percentage table.

A **correlations table** highlights the strength of the relationship between different variables. In Table 3, we see a table that has the *variable labels* for the rows and *number labels* for the columns. The numbers as column headers correspond to the variables numbered on the left side of the table. Thus, we see that the intersection between row 1 (math test score) and column 1 is 1.00 because the correlation of a variable with itself is perfect at 1. To read this table, one has to look at the intersection of the variables and this becomes the correlation coefficient.

Thus, we see that the correlation between math test score (number 1 on the column) and reading test score (number 2 on the row) is 0.88, which means these two variables are strongly *positively correlated*. The higher the score in math, the higher the score in reading. We also see that math and reading test scores do not have a correlation with age, at 0.12 and 0.08 respectively. However, we see that there are suggestive *negative correlations* between test scores and being absent during a month. It means that the more absences one has in a month, the lower the test scores may be on average.

Table 4. Regression on math test scores, n = 1406 students

	Model 1	Model 2	Model 3
Absence per month	-0.55*** (0.04)	-0.46*** (0.03)	-0.53*** (0.04)
Reading test score		0.23** (0.06)	
Age			0.02 (0.01)
Intercept	50.78*** (0.23)	53.64*** (0.24)	51.39*** (0.23)

Source: Education Survey of 2018

Notes: The table shows regression coefficients of math test score on independent variables. Standard errors are written in parentheses.
* $p < 0.05$, ** $p < 0.01$, *** $p < 0.001$

Some things that may also be good to note with this table is that the numbers **align at the decimal point**, and that only until two decimal points are included. This helps your reader see at first glance the relationships you hope to emphasize. If your table has fewer than two rows and two columns, you can forego a table and just use a textual description. If it takes too much time to decipher your table, you may have to split your table.[60]

A **regression table** shows the effect on the dependent variable of a one-unit addition in the independent variable. In Model 1 of Table 4, we see that an addition of one day of absence (*independent variable*) is significantly related to a 0.55-point decrease in one's math test score (*dependent variable*). The statistical significance is denoted by the three asterisks after the number (-0.55***). Model 2 adds *reading test score* as a covariate or control variable, and a one-point addition in reading test score is also associated with increasing the students' math test score. Model 3 adds another covariate, which is *age* and this does not have any influence on the dependent variable. In all three models, absence is associated with lower test scores in math. You will note that there are also things written inside parentheses and these are the standard errors, or the standard deviation of a sampling distribution.[61]

When creating your regression table, here are some ideas to note:

1. Write on the title what is the **dependent variable** you are regressing. In the example above, the dependent variable is math test score.
2. Do not forget to write the **statistical significance**, commonly denoted by the number of asterisks after the coefficient. Additionally, write the legend for statistical significance at the bottom of the table.
3. **Order** and **group** the variables such that they follow a logical sequence. The "Absence per month" variable is at the top because this is the main independent variable; the two covariates follow because of the order they will show up in models 2 and 3. If you have more covariates, it will be wise to group your covariates for those that have similar characteristics (e.g. grouping demographic details together).

With the ideas written here, I hope you have found how to **more effectively and deliberately use tables**. Generally, the principles are similar to figures when you should make tables easy and intuitive to read. Tables should support your results, and oftentimes, less is actually more with your tables. Focus on data that are connected to your main research question and argument, without hiding data that fail to support your thesis. Learning to show tabular data properly will go a long way in helping you explain your results.

4.4 Absent or unrelated data explanation

After creating figures and tables that form the foundation of your results section, you will have to create a **complementary text** that will let your readers know which details to focus on. There are a couple of mistakes that can happen when writing the text of your results section. First, you may think that since the data are already on the figures and tables, you no longer need to write the text and you simply proceed to an interpretation of the results. You will still need to write the text, however, so that your reader may know which ideas or numbers are important and should be focused on.

A second mistake is the opposite of the first one when you try to **describe everything** written in your table. The complementary text should be there to highlight your points so that your reader will know what to focus on when you interpret the data. You do not need to talk about the significance of each of the numbers present in your tables. For example, you do not need to write the correlations of all the variables but you will have to highlight the correlations that are significant and that advance or challenge your thesis. When you talk about the regression tables, you do not need to write about the coefficients for each of the independent variables and covariates. You need only to talk about the coefficients that are significant and related to your research argument.

A third common mistake is the **disorganization** in your results section, especially when ideas jump from one table to another, or from one figure to another. When writing the results section, it is important to move the ideas chronologically from the first table or figure to the next one. Another issue that may cause confusion or disorganization is when you fail to write which table you are referring to. To help your readers know which they should focus on, it will be necessary to include pointers like "Table 1 shows that…," "Model 1 of Table 2 highlights how…," or "Figure 3 displays the…" You may also wish to devote a singular paragraph just for the discussion of a table or figure since having one paragraph for two tables or figures may cause confusion in your reader. By organizing and referring to the tables and figures, you help your reader know which idea to focus on so that they know these form your evidence for your interpretation later on.

When writing the results section, here are some things you should write: **sample size** to show how many were included in your sample, **means** and **standard deviations** for continuous variables, **percentages** or **percentage point differences** for categorical variables or pie charts, **downward or upward trends** for graphs, **correlation coefficients** with its consequent meaning for your argument, and **regression coefficients** with their ***p-values*** and meaning. Examples of sentences that you would see in the results section include:

- Figure 4 shows an upward trend in the publication of books and journals from 1991 to 2009. In 1991, book publication was only at 100 books per year and journal article publication was only at 70 articles per year. However, in 2009, book and article publications were at 385 and 360, respectively.
- Table 1 shows that math test scores have a mean value of 70.22 with minimum and maximum values of 40 and 92, respectively. However, reading test scores have a lower mean and less dispersion with its mean value of 65.33 and range of 58 to 81.
- Table 2 presents people's level of agreement or disagreement with the statements on research competency. Of the 1406 students surveyed, more than half (59.03%) agreed that they can do research—these are people who agreed and strongly agreed in the first statement in the survey.
- Table 3 provides correlations coefficients with the strongest positive correlation between math and reading test scores at 0.88. The strongest negative correlations can be seen between reading test score and school absence at -0.66, and between math test score and school absence at -0.53. This suggest that the more absence a student has, the higher the likelihood that the student has low test scores on both subjects.
- Regression results are provided in Table 4, with the three models showing that absence from school is a statistically significant predictor of lower math test scores. The first model does not have any covariates while the subsequent ones add reading test score and age as covariates.

Some other tips and cautions might help as you write your research paper. Be careful about using **causal language**. Just because something is correlated, or has a statistically significant regression coefficient, does not immediately mean that the independent variable *causes* the dependent variable. In the social sciences, you need randomized controlled studies to ascertain causation, and this may not be feasible in your research. However, you may use words like *influence*, *predict*, and *is associated with* to show the significant relationship between two variables. For example, you can say that "Absence from school *influences* math test scores, with every one day of absence associated, on average, with a 0.53-point decrease in one's math test score." In this example, nowhere was it said that absence causes lower math scores but that it influences the decrease in the score.

Another idea to keep in mind when writing the results section is to not interpret your results but rather to provide evidence for your interpretation and discussion that will come later in your paper. You should think of your results section as a space for you to accumulate firsthand evidence, organize it, and refer to it when you have your research argument.

Lastly, you should end your results section with a short paragraph that synthesizes your key findings. You should highlight the most important results your readers will need to remember as they read the discussion section. This is particularly important if you have a lot of information, and hope your readers can remember the key ones, which are necessary evidence for your argument.[62]

4.5 Incorrect use of quotes

If quantitative research uses numerical data, tables, and figures, qualitative research utilizes **quotations**, **texts**, and **observations** as sources of its data. These will often come from your observation notes or from your interview transcripts, and they serve as primary evidence for the conclusions you make for your research.

When writing the result section of your research, there are a couple of mistakes that can be committed. One is when there are **too many quotes** so the whole results section seems to be a string of quotations; the other is the opposite–having **too few quotes** so the reader does not know which ideas came from the author and which ones came from the informants. Below is an example of the first scenario:

> Research about using technology in the classroom has shown that students are interested in it. One student said, "I really like doing

> online activities…." Another student remarked, "There are many things I like about technology but I also think that it can be a distraction…." A third student said, "The best use of technology is when we do activities where we can get real-time feedback…" A fourth student said….

In the given example, it seems as if the quotes were simply dropping from the sky, and the researcher was just trying to fill up the pages with direct quotes. When a student writes quote after quote—even worse, block quote after block quote—it will seem to the teacher that the student just wants to have page fillers. To clarify, **regular quotes** are quotes that are within quotation marks ("…") inside the paragraph while **block quotes** are quotes that start on their own line because they are usually longer and span more lines. In the manual of the American Psychological Association, quotations that are 40 words or more should be in block format. When writing block quotes, the entire quotation is indented 0.5 inches from the left (the same indentation for the start of a new paragraph).[63]

When a research is filled with quotations without any structure, the results section seems like a tapestry of cut-and-pasted quotes from different people. There have even been times when researchers wrote long block quotes from one person, and then moved to another long block quote from another person. One of the ways to address this mistake is by **uncovering themes or structures** that hold together the answers of your informants. For a research on educational technology, you may have themes on technology's being advantageous, its being a distraction to students, and teachers' reluctance to use it.

When writing a regular quote, consider this example:

> One theme from the interview with students and teachers is the acknowledgement of the benefits of using educational technology. Of the twelve people interviewed, most had positive remarks about educational technology's usefulness. A senior high school student said, "*Natutuwa ako sa paggamit ng bagong teknolohiya kasi mas nape-prepare ako sa trabaho* [I find using new technologies

> helpful because I get better prepared for work outside]." Another informant, a science teacher, remarked how technology helps her in giving feedback to students.

Notice that the paragraph started with a discussion of the **theme** or the **abstract idea** that encapsulates what some people have said. After this, there is the discussion of how people provided answers that related to the theme. In this part, you can write about the context of your respondents or how many of the respondents had answers that were related to the theme. When writing the quote, you should introduce the person speaking whether by providing a name, a fake name, or a general descriptor.

If you plan to quote someone **verbatim**, you should put the words inside quotation marks. If your respondent uses the local language when your paper uses English, it will be important to put in *italics* the local language and have the translation inside square brackets [ ]. If only some words are in the local language you may just automatically supply the translation in the square brackets without doing a translation of the whole statement. To diversify your ways of quoting, it may also be good to **paraphrase** or **summarize** some quotes or ideas from your informant. In the last sentence of the previous example, the idea of the science teacher was no longer quoted but just summarized. These are just some ways to deal with too many or too few quotes.

Another way of addressing this is by effectively using block quotations. Sometimes, block quotations are **long answers** that have to be quoted at length. There are a number of reasons for preferring to do block quotes: (1) you want your informants' **natural "voice"** to be heard, (2) paraphrasing the informants' answers will lead to **inaccurate substitutes**, or (3) there are **terms**, **words**, or **images** that you want captured in the quote. Whatever your reason, you have to deliberately use block quotes, and not simply use them when you need to meet minimum page requirements. Another way of using block quotes is by quoting a conversation between the informant and the researcher:

One of the themes from the interviews is the distraction that students experience when using technology. In one interview, John speaks of how technology can lead him to feel unfocused on the task at hand:

> John: Because we use our laptops in school, it's so easy to go to Facebook.
> Interviewer: Why don't you just disable your internet then?
> John: When I see other people using Facebook on their laptop, it somehow gives me permission to use my internet.
> Interviewer: What is the effect of this on you?
> John: I find it harder to focus on the lesson and the tasks given because I get easily distracted...

From the example, the **block quote format** was used for the conversation between the researcher and informant, and it provided a way for the conversation to be "heard" by the readers of the research. When quoting the interview conversation, you must know which sections have to be quoted since it is unnecessary to quote the whole conversation.

When working with qualitative research, it will be important to create a structure or clarify the set of themes that emerge from the interviews and observations. When using quotes, you have to strike a balance between having too much and too few quotes, and this can be addressed with being deliberate about the use of regular and block quotes, and of paraphrasing answers. One last mistake that can come is when **quotes come out of nowhere**:

> There are many things that can bring distraction for students. "At present, the paradigmatic example of a tempting off-task website is Facebook, but as the popularity of this website decreases, students may move to other websites like Instagram or Twitter."[64]

In the example, it seemed as if the quote just fell from the sky without any introduction or context. This is a common mistake with beginning researchers who think that just because they have the citation at the endnote or footnote, they no longer need to introduce the quote. However, introducing the quote or the idea is necessary so that readers are not caught off guard with your assertions. Providing the context helps them know where the quote is literally and figuratively coming from.

4.6 Non-identified informants

A related mistake associated with quotes that fall out of nowhere is when you fail to **identify the participants** you have in your qualitative research. There are times when researchers just write, "One person said this... another person said that..." There seems to be no details about who the persons are. On the one hand, if you told your informant that they will be anonymous in your study, you have to respect this but this does not mean that you should not disclose any detail about the person. To describe someone as an employee or an entrepreneur will go a long way when readers make sense of your informants' answers.

Admittedly, there are two extremes when referring to informants' identities. On one end is when you have **no information** about your informants while on the other end is when you have **too much information** that your participants are no longer anonymous. In this section, I talk about strategies to help give more life and embodiment to your research informants without breaking confidentiality.

For quotes from other **researchers** or **authors**, you will have to introduce who the person is. Is she a sociologist? a psychologist? a Harvard professor? a writer? Since books and journal articles are public, you do not need to hide the author's name or identity. You only have to be sure that their affiliations and identities are correct. For example, you may refer to an author as a professor from the University of the Philippines when she is already with Kyoto University. In this sense, you will have to refer to the status of the researcher or author at the time of your writing the research.

For quotes from **government officials**, **celebrities**, and other **public personalities**, it is often the case that they are identified in the research paper. The assumption is that you are interviewing them because of their position and not just because of their personal circumstances. When writing about their responses, you have to identify the person's name and their current public identity. Is the person an actor or a politician? Is he a mayor of a certain place? Or is she the chief of police of a certain region? You also have to show how their public identities could affect their answers and which of their identities are most salient for your own research questions.

For quotes that come from your **research respondents**, you will have to also provide background details that may be pertinent to your research. Is the informant a student? a teacher? a high school dropout? a technology expert? What is the gender of your participant? By providing these details, you are helping your readers understand what could be driving the answers people give. Some writers will provide pseudonyms, and you just have to clarify this at the start by saying something like, "Names were changed to protect the participants' confidentiality…" Aside from changing names of individuals, another way of protecting confidentiality is by changing the name of the community or institution (e.g. town or school) particularly if there are issues that might compromise it. In either case, you should clearly say in the footnote or in the body that some details have been changed to protect the safety and confidentiality of informants.

4.7 Plagiarism

The problem with plagiarism exists not only when presenting the results or interpreting them, but can actually occur at any point of the research paper—or even the entire research paper altogether. Broadly, plagiarism is the **passing off** of another person's ideas or words as one's own or the usage of these ideas or words **without credit** to the originator. At the core of plagiarism is theft and fraud—of stealing someone's idea (whether intentionally or not) and lying about it afterward. In most cases, the act is usually considered cheating and it is often difficult to pinpoint intentionality. This means that it is often challenging to separate when plagiarism is a deliberate act on the part of the researcher to gain advantage, or when the researcher just does not know better.[65]

One of the misconceptions about plagiarism is that it is just when you copy someone else's ideas and not cite them. However, there are many **different types** and **levels** of actions that are considered plagiarism. In an article in *Higher Education Research and Development,* John Walker describes a continuum of seven behaviors considered plagiarism:

- **Sham paraphrasing** happens when a researcher *copies* the material verbatim (word for word) and *cites* the source, but represents the idea as paraphrased since the quote is not placed inside quotation marks.
- **Illicit paraphrasing** happens when a researcher *paraphrases* the material but does *not acknowledge* the source of the material.
- **Verbatim copying** happens when a researcher *copies* verbatim the material *without acknowledging* the source.
- **Self-plagiarism** or **recycling** happens when one submits an assignment *more than once*, or when one *uses a previous work* without citing that it was used in a different paper or context.
- **Ghostwriting** happens when *someone else* does a paper (even if just part of the paper) and the work is represented as solely one's own.
- **Other plagiarism** happens when one's material is *copied* from another person *with the knowledge* of that other person.
- **Purloining** happens when one's material is *copied* from another person *without the knowledge* of that other person.[66]

From these examples, we see there are many variations of plagiarism and you should definitely familiarize yourself with the different ways that plagiarism can happen. This knowledge is helpful whether you are a teacher, a student, or a researcher since it provides you with **clear descriptions** of what constitute plagiarism apart from merely copying information and not acknowledging the source.

Aside from the ones mentioned above, these other things are still considered plagiarism: (1) failing to put in quotation marks when the section is a verbatim quote, (2) giving wrong information about the source of the quotation or providing incorrect reference, (3) changing the words (e.g. getting synonyms of words) but essentially keeping sentence structure and making it seem that the idea was paraphrased, and (4) copying so many words from the original source that it almost seems like a verbatim quote.[67] These too are subtle ways when plagiarism can happen.

So how do you **avoid plagiarism**? First is really about being familiar with what actions can be considered plagiarism. Most people, for example, do not know that there is such a thing as *self-plagiarism* when one uses one's own idea without acknowledging it from a previous written source. Becoming familiar with the various ways plagiarism can be done hopefully helps the person become more aware of one's unintentional mistakes. Although knowing a mistake does not mean that one will automatically avoid the mistake, the awareness should at least shake someone from complacency and not excuse the person with ignorance. To know that there are other ways of plagiarism aside from Ctrl C + Ctrl V (Copy - Paste) means that people are knowledgeable of the standards for academic integrity.

The other way of avoiding plagiarism is by simply **citing** where your information came from. This could be done through in-text citations that tell your readers where you obtained the idea. For example,

> In the twentieth century, the United States' social climate has evolved from one where there a lot of opportunities for social cohesion and connection to one where there has been greater individualism and disconnection (Putnam, 2000).

Here, the sentence tells the reader that the idea came from Robert Putnam who published a book entitled *Bowling Alone: The Collapse and Revival of American Community*.[68] The in-text citation of "(Putnam, 2000)" highlights that the idea does not come from the one presently writing but from someone else. To know more details about the author, you will need to write a reference list, which provides more details in addition to the author's last name and date of publication. Whether you use the citation style of the American Psychological Association or the Chicago Manual of Style, the reference list usually includes the authors' full name, full article or book titles, and the date and place of publication.[69]

Other ways of doing in-text citation include:

> According to Putnam (2000), US life…
> Putnam (2000) argues/highlights/suggests/provides…
> In the book *Bowling Alone,* Putnam (2000) shows that….

These examples are for in-text citation but there are other ways of citing. If you are using the **notes style** of the Chicago Manual, you should write a footnote (or endnote) with the details mentioned above. The proper ways of citing and writing the reference will be discussed in detail in the next chapter.

Aside from the knowledge of the types of plagiarism and the use of citations and references, another way of avoiding plagiarism is by **assessing** which of your ideas need to backed or seem to have been said by someone else. You may think that your idea is unique but someone may have suggested it already, so it will be good practice to see if someone else has said something similar. You will also have to assess if your **paraphrasing** was correctly done—that is, you got the main idea and used your own words—and that you still acknowledge the source of your paraphrase. If you plan to use the words of the original author, be sure to also place them within quotation marks.

Avoiding plagiarism is very important since committing this mistake can have grave consequences on your grade, or worse, your reputation. One of the difficulties with judging plagiarism is that it is often hard to know the intentions of the researcher for plagiarizing, and the punishment is usually meted out because of the act rather than the intention. Hopefully, knowing the various ways plagiarism happens, being informed of how to cite sources, and assessing your own written work help you avoid this costly mistake.

4.8 Absent or unclear discussion section

After writing the results section, you might think that you can just write the conclusion since you have already given your evidence for your research. However, your evidence will mean nothing if you do not make an effort at interpreting the results. This interpretation is the essence of the discussion section since this section provides a space for you to connect evidence with your main research argument. It is a space for:

- reminding the reader about the research **question**, **argument**, and **importance**;
- **synthesizing findings**, and understanding the deeper meaning of your results;
- connecting your results to **broader insights** from your discipline or your topic; and
- noting unexpected ideas, and considering **alternative explanations** of findings.[70]

As hinted, one common mistake is to just let the results section stand on its own without a discussion of its meaning. To take a food analogy, this is like giving people clean vegetables without making the effort to cook it. Although your readers may make something of your results, you did not make the effort to direct them on how to understand the results. Thus, you should find ways to make more sense of your findings and evidence—use them so that readers will have an informed understanding of your research.

Connected to this mistake is the fact that some discussion sections are just **repetitions** of the results section: they can just reiterate what was already known, what the themes were, or what the numbers were. During these cases, it is important to know what distinguishes the results section from the discussion section. For quantitative research, the results section usually provides the tables and evidence that readers should focus on while the discussion section highlights how the numbers relate to the research argument. The discussion no longer needs to mention detailed means or coefficients (this should have been in the results), but just describe the data broadly and how this can be interpreted for your research. If your research is about how absences have negative effects on academic achievement, your discussion section should no longer say what the coefficients are but talk about what could be the mechanisms or reasons behind such effects.

For qualitative research, the results section usually presents the themes, responses, and quotes from the respondents while the discussion section tries to highlight the **deeper meaning and structure** to those themes. Similar to quantitative research, there is no longer any need to quote your informants in the discussion section; only the broad ideas or themes from the quotes are used to answer the main research question. If your research is about the effects of educational technologies on students and teachers, you need not repeat the themes that were mentioned but you may focus on the differences in response between students and teachers, or the bigger issues of distraction or institutional readiness to technologies. In both cases, the discussion should be focused less on the data and more on the research question. Your discussion should explain your data, not repeat your data.

One way of helping explain your data is by referring to **previous research** and comparing the results—those that align with your findings and those that challenge what you discover. Again, a common mistake that people make with the discussion section is to forego previous research because they think that this should just be in the literature review. Inasmuch as your discussion should not be a repetition of your literature review, it should also not be absent of what others have already discovered.

So how do you use previous studies? One way is to use the findings from other studies to support your findings. You can highlight how other studies actually confirm what you discovered and that what you discovered actually happens in other contexts. Another way is to compare the findings from other research with your research findings. You can show how there are some differences in your findings and that these differences could add nuance to the topic of your research. A third way of using previous studies is by challenging the results of these studies and providing alternative explanations that your results give evidence to. You can say that there are inaccuracies with former studies that are challenged by the present study. Lastly, previous studies may be used to connect your results to broader themes in the literature. You can present how your research is more meaningful and relevant when related to a broader topic.

Be careful, however, of using the discussion section as a place for you to talk about your **personal opinion** on the topic. Your discussion should always be based on the results, evidence and current literature, and "over-interpreting" happens when you go beyond your data—mixing the data you have with your personal considerations and opinions. To address this mistake, you should reflect about your selection and interpretation of data—careful that you are not adding ideas that are not supported by the research or being swayed by your personal biases. When you have written your discussion section, you should be critical about how much of your interpretation is actually supported by data.[71] If you find that most of your interpretation is supported by data (yours and others), that should be a good sign.

Similarly, be careful about making **sweeping generalizations** about your data since your research may just be limited to the people you sampled. Again, inasmuch as it is crucial to see how your insights can be applied more generally, you must not make it seem that your insights can be applied to all situations. It will be good to talk about the conceptual lessons and practical applications of your research, but to argue that this is the definitive answer is naïve and irresponsible.

In this case, it will be wise to write and be transparent about the **limitations** of your research. Some limitations may include conceptual limitations if you were unable to answer some of the research questions you initially set out to investigate, or if your insights are limited and cannot be generalized to other contexts. Some limitations may include methodological limitations if there were data unobtained, methods unemployed, or problems met while conducting the research. Now, you might ask why you need to point out these limitations. The reality is that your readers will be as smart as—if not smarter than—you, and they may point out the limitations of your research if you fail to talk about them yourself. Thus, it is a good idea to just be forthright and transparent about your research's limitations.

Thus, it will be good to remember that your discussion section should have these components:

- your research question and argument;
- summary and explanation of your findings;
- connection with previous literature or other studies;
- alternative explanations and possible response to counterarguments;
- acknowledgement of limitations and suggestions for further study; and
- a conclusion that talks about the broader ideas and practical applications of the present study.

4.9 Inability to engage counterarguments

When you write an academic or research paper, you are often providing your reader an argument or thesis, and this argument is something that the reader may either subscribe to or not. Your results and discussion section should provide your reader with the evidence and reasoning that back up the arguments you make. As has been said, to say something obvious does not merit the effort used for doing a full research, and so your reader must have some room to doubt your argument. When this happens, your reader will have a **counterargument**, or a possible argument against your main thesis, logic, or evidence.

Although a counterargument is not necessary in a research paper, it will be good for you to anticipate possible **opposing opinions** people will have about your research. If you argue that absences can influence academic performance, your reader may argue that both absence and academic performance are influenced by the students' personal motivation. If you argue that students should not use educational technologies because they can cause distraction, your reader may argue that there are a number of research findings that actually argue the opposite. If you have these diverging views from your readers, how will you address their legitimate differences in opinion?

It is often a good sign when your research elicits opposing views from your readers because this means that your research is challenging something significant in how people view the world. Of course, this also means that you will need to be more persuasive in your argumentation: Do you have a clear thesis statement? Is your reasoning sound? Are there data and evidence to support your reasoning? One aspect included in persuasive argumentation but often forgotten is how you **respond to counterarguments.** You will have to assess how a skeptical reader might read your research and raise doubts and objections.

But why provide counterarguments and respond to these? Think of it in terms of the difference between speaking and writing. When you speak (or debate) with a person *in person*, you have the opportunity to clarify your ideas and respond if someone has a question. However, when you write something, your paper will have to speak for itself and you are not there to engage with your reader personally. Thus, if your reader has questions or doubts, you do not have the opportunity to defend your arguments. But if you anticipate doubts, objections, concerns, and counterarguments, you may write these down and respond to them individually before your reader even raises them.

To do this in your discussion section, you first have to be critical about your research and find the likely objection to your reasoning. You can talk about how there can be a different set of conclusions to be made with the data at hand, or how there are alternative explanations to your research. You need only to think about how a skeptical reader might think about your research differently.

When you have written the possible doubts or objections, you will have to respond to the counterargument by **refuting** them. You have to show how the counterargument is itself **flawed, incomplete, mistaken**, or **equally possible**. In a way, even if you have engaged in doubting your research, you still have to argue why there is a solid basis for accepting the conclusions you make in your research. You should not end by talking about the doubts that people will have of your research since you have to show how your argument still stands despite the objections some people have.

As with everything about research mistakes, be careful about using this too much or too often. The inclusion of counterarguments and refutations helps your reader see that you thought deeply about the topic. However, having too many twists and turns in your research will likely make them ask if you are clear about what your research argument is.

4.10 Research question remains unanswered

When you are about to finish your research, you will notice substantial development or changes from when you initially started. You may have to have new data sources because certain data are not available to you; you may have to change your original title because it is no longer applicable; you may have to shift your thesis statement because you learned new things in the process of research. It is usually taken as a good sign that you make changes in a research because this means that there are new insights forming and there is a deeper understanding of the topic at hand.

When you make changes, however, you have to make sure that these changes are **consistent** across the document. If you change your sources, it should be reflected in your methods section. If your research has a new focus, it should be reflected in the title and other sections. If your thesis statement changes, you will have to modify your introduction, literature review, and discussion. Your review of the document is important to ensure that things connect as one whole document.

One mistake that comes when making research changes is that the **research question remains unanswered**. Because of the many new information and insights obtained, you might change the direction of your research. When this happens, you will have to periodically ask yourself if what you are writing is addressing your original research question. It might be possible that the new insights are no longer connected to your earlier question, and you will have to make changes either in your study or in your question.

When faced with this mistake of the research question being left unanswered, there are one of two ways of fixing it. One option is to go back to your data, and see which ones connect with your original research question. The other option is to change the question of your research to make it connect with the data you obtained. Both options are actually time- and energy-consuming, and so it is much better to be preventive about it.

To prevent this from happening, it will be good to periodically ask oneself at different points of the research process if the original research question is being answered. It will be a good idea to assess your research if its direction is answering your main question. If it does not, you will have to make decisions on whether to pursue the original question or ask another one. When you are able to reflect periodically about the status of your research, you will be able to assess how faithfully you are answering the main research question.

CHAPTER 5

MISTAKES IN WRITING

Mistakes can happen at different points in the research process, and even the best researchers can still make mistakes when it comes to the writing portion. After all, writing a research is markedly different from writing personal essays, short stories, or poems. There is need for brevity and directness in research writing, as well as for a formal tone.

In this chapter, we talk about mistakes in the writing of the research, whether these be big mistakes in terms of voice and structure, or minute details in terms of inaccurate words or punctuations. The chapter will also talk about common mistakes in citations and how to address these when writing the research. Learning these mistakes can provide you a checklist after you write your research; you can use this checklist to see if you made those mistakes and thus make changes.

5.1 Informal tone and language

Research writing is an academic exercise and will need a **tone** and a **language appropriate** to its academic nature. However, appropriate academic language should not be understood as an imperative or an excuse for boring writing since there are ways of making formal writing engaging while objective. There are a few issues and questions regarding tone and language:

- Should I use first-person or third-person pronouns?
- How do I avoid making it sound like a personal opinion?
- What "tones" are inappropriate for research?
- How do I express ideas more precisely?

For pronouns, you have the option of using the first person (I/We) or the third person (He/She/They) to refer to the researcher/s. Usually the **second person** (You) is not used because the research paper should not directly address the reader; the second-person pronouns are usually used with guide books (like the one you are holding), manuals, cookbooks, or articles that need to engage directly with the reader.

So in a published research, when do we use a first-person pronoun and when is the third-person pronoun appropriate? Here are some examples of their use:

> First person: In this research, *I* argue that higher carbon dioxide emissions…
> Third person: The *researcher* tests the assumptions, and *she* shows that…

Both are actually acceptable, but there are differences in preferences—and the choice between the two can be a hotly debated topic among researchers. In academic essays in schools, teachers usually advise students to stick to the **objective-sounding third person** pronoun since using the I/We pronouns can make students sound as if they are storytelling or expressing a personal opinion. However, it must also be noted that the American Psychological Association actually recommends using the **first-person pronoun** for a number of reasons and circumstances to be explained later.[72]

Of course, there are a number of considerations that will affect your decision, like your subject or discipline, your school or adviser's preference, or your own preference—so it is probably best to consult with your peers. For the purposes of providing you with options, I show some mistakes when the first-person pronoun is not preferred:

> *I think that* learning a second language is important for high school students.
> *In my opinion*, the Philippine economy is growing at a steady pace.
> *As scientists, we believe* environmental problems need to be addressed more urgently.

In these examples, the use of the personal pronoun I or we actually made it seem as if it was mainly about the person's ideas or opinions, and not about the facts or evidence. If you are the reader, you may probably find that these research papers are influenced by the authors' personal feelings and biases—which may or may not be supported by evidence. One way of addressing this is by taking out the words in italics, and just dropping the words that refer to the researcher.

But when do you use first person pronouns? Here are some suggestions from the American Psychological Association's manual of style:

1. **Avoid ambiguity**. Usually, the word "the author/researcher" will be used to refer to the person writing the research. However, if this is preceded by the research of other authors, this may lead to ambiguity. For example, you write "Mueller and Abrutyn (2015) highlight suicidality, and *the researchers* further clarify this position." In this example, it is not clear who "the researchers" are referring to—Mueller and Abrutyn or the authors? In this example, the first-person pronoun is preferred.
2. **Clarify passive construction.** Writers who are staying clear of first-person pronouns usually write sentences in the passive voice, which happens when the subject is not acting but is being acted upon by the verb. For example, "The research was conducted in Cebu's urban center." Although there is nothing grammatically wrong, the active voice is usually clearer and sounds better. Thus, you can rewrite the sentence as "I conducted the research in Cebu's urban center."
3. **Emphasize positionality.** In qualitative research, it is important to clarify your position or relationship with your informants. In this way, it will be helpful to use the personal pronouns to show what is your connection to the people who are informing you. This also helps clarify when you are making an interpretation of the data.

4. **Avoid anthropomorphism.** Anthropomorphism happens when animals or inanimate objects are accorded human traits, behavior, or emotions. Sometimes, to avoid using the first-person pronoun, researchers say "The research attempts experiments...." In this example, an inanimate object (the research) is attempting experiments, which is a human action. Since this sounds illogical, it is best to just use the first-person pronoun to refer to what the researcher is doing.

When using the first person, you have to be careful by using it sparingly and strategically. Using I or we much more than necessary may actually distract your readers and may make it seem that the focus of the research is your interpretation.

Whatever is your choice between the first-person or the third-person pronoun, it will be important to be consistent in your document. If you start by referring to yourself as "the researchers," it is necessary to use "they" as pronoun. If you refer to yourself as "I" (or "we" if you have co-authors), you will need to use this consistently.

Another mistake is when the tone of the research is **inappropriate**. Here are some examples when the tone of the research may be inappropriate:

1. The education department should stop the implementation of its new reform.
2. We are certain about the effectiveness of the new intervention.
3. There are several options for reform.
4. The third reform is a fantastic option to help improve education.

The first example has an **obligating tone**, where it seems that you are forcing someone to do an action. Your research is not a place where you tell people what they are obliged to do (e.g. *should stop*) since research is primarily about telling people what is rather than what should be. You may write recommendations at the end of the research but you have to be careful about making it seem that your research is forcing people to a certain way of thinking or acting. For the sentence example, it can be transformed to "Based on the evidence, it is recommended for the education department to stop the implementation of its new reform." In this way, it does not seem that you are directing what the education department should do, but you are simply giving an informed recommendation.

The second example has a very **direct tone**, which conveys 100% certainty in the argument. This direct tone actually sounds a little presumptuous, especially when no alternatives are considered or there is no room for dissenting opinions. When you see that your research has this very direct tone, you should think about how you can be more tentative in your tone. This does not mean that you have to be unsure about your research, but it does mean that you are humble in being open to other explanations, ideas, and arguments. The second sentence can then be transformed to: "A number of researchers have expressed their agreement with the effectiveness of the intervention." This still gives the same idea but is more toned down.

In the third example, the word "several" shows an **inaccurate tone**. When writing research, it is important to be specific and explicit in the expression of your ideas. Some common mistakes involving inaccuracy include "several," "majority of the population," "some years ago," "a number of researchers," and "few writers." To address this, it is best to clarify the number, estimate, or range of the items described. Instead of saying that there are several options, you can say that there are three options. Instead of saying that the majority of the students want a four-day workweek, you can say that around 60 percent of students want it. Instead of saying something happened some years ago, you can say that it happened around 8 to 10 years ago. Being more accurate helps your readers quantify and qualify your research.

The use of the word "fantastic" in the fourth example makes the sentence have a more **dramatic or exaggerated tone**. The use of intensifiers, like *awfully*, *very*, *really*, *amazing*, and *super*, can be quite distracting for your reader. It can also signal that you are mixing your evidence with your own biases and personal opinion. When you use these words that exaggerate certain claims, it seems as if you are no longer balanced in your judgment of what you are researching on. Thus, it is best to avoid using these words that can suggest your prejudice and weaken your credibility.

When working with research, there are a couple of mistakes that you will have to be careful with: having inconsistent use of pronouns, using too many first-person pronouns, or using tones that are obligating, direct, inaccurate, or exaggerated. It is important to recognize how these mistakes can affect how your readers perceive the objectivity of your research.

5.2 Unclear point

Have you ever read a research paper, or even just a paragraph, and came away thinking you did not get the whole point of what you just read? Sometimes it seems as if the writer wants you to read between the lines; unfortunately, research is not the best place for people to read between the lines. For most research, either it is written in the text itself or it is not. So how do you get your point across clearly?

In any unit of discourse (a paragraph, a chapter, a section, a whole research), there is always the **index/ starting position** and the **ending position**. The former helps *structure* what is about to be read while the latter helps *recapitulate* what was said in a longer unit of discourse (e.g. conclusion for the whole research). Although having index and ending positions are not necessary for every unit of discourse, understanding their dynamics can help you write more clearly since you take into consideration how your reader will need to anticipate what you are about to say or remember what you just said.

For a paragraph, the beginning sentence should help orient your reader about what you will say. This is often called your point or your thesis for that paragraph. One example of an effective use of the index position is:

> Indigenous peoples are experiencing a number of challenges, including socioeconomic, cultural, and environmental concerns. In terms of their socioeconomic position, their current source of income—farming—is unable to sustain the needs of the family, and this is made worse since a number of people take advantage of the indigenous people's lack of formal education. Culturally, the people's traditional artifacts and practices are being eroded and are not being documented; more and more people prefer to live in the same way as lowlanders. Environmentally, they are always on the edge because of the threat of eviction by mega-projects, or the pollution that comes from cities that emerge near their ancestral lands.

In the example, the first sentence orients the reader that there are at least three concerns that indigenous people have: socioeconomic, cultural, and environmental. The paragraph then goes on to describe in detail what each of these concerns means. At the end of the paragraph, you will notice that the point was not repeated since you do not need to make the point twice in a paragraph as the index is still quite fresh. For longer units of discourse (e.g. section or chapter), it may be necessary to have an ending point to recapitulate what you said.

This example shows one way of using index positions, which must help **establish your readers' expectations**. For a paragraph, your first sentence should provide a way of saying or summarizing what is discussed in that paragraph. For a chapter or section, your first paragraph should organize what you will say and it should make the whole chapter or section coherent. For a research paper, your introduction must clarify what the entire argument is.

Of course, there are ways of having index positions said **explicitly** (I argue that.../ We investigate how.../ The results show three themes....), and also more **subtle** ways of just giving a taste of what will appear much later. If you do not know your main point, whether in your paragraph or in your research, it will be quite difficult for your readers to also be informed about your argument. One way that helps create effective index positions is through the identification of themes or key words in your discourse. When writing a paragraph, what are the most important words in it that can help orient your reader to your paragraph? When writing a research, what are the main ideas that help orient the structure and movement of your whole research?

To test whether you are clear on your point, you should pass the **underline test**. If a person asks you to underline the point of your whole research, will you be able to underline a thesis statement? If a person asks you to point out the main idea of a paragraph, will you be able to highlight what it is without much effort? The key here is that your point should appear on the written document and should not be something that the reader will have to mysteriously figure out. There is no such thing as an implicit point.

More than being explicit about your point, articulating it clearly will also help you **structure** your ideas and the **movement** of your ideas. Your readers will want to know where you are taking them, and this is one of the primary functions of your index position. One mistake that some researchers commit is that they have an index position but the discussion does not follow through on what was "promised" in the index position. It is as if you are telling readers to expect one thing in your point but you give a totally different one in your discussion. To address this, always make sure that you read your index again and assess if it connects with the discussion you have just written.

In academic writing, however, you will know that the insights often come after or in the process of writing. Sometimes, it is difficult to know your point clearly because it is only as you write that you also clarify what your main ideas are. Thus, the problem is that the points can often come in last—not by design, but by accident. When faced with this problem, the best solution is to revise your index position so that it reflects what transpired as you wrote the discussion section. Although it is alright to reserve your main point at the end, you will still have to provide guides or themes at the index position so that your readers will know what to expect and how to read your discussion.

5.3 Unconnected paragraphs and sentences

Now that you know how to work on your point for every unit of discourse (e.g. paragraph), it will be important to know how to make your other ideas connect with the point—that is, how to make your **sentences connect to the index** position, and make **sentences connect with each other**. A common mistake is often that certain paragraphs and sentences do not flow naturally from one to the other. For example,

> The EDSA People Power Revolution happened in 1986. There were many factors that contributed to people going to Camp Crame and EDSA. The goal is to oust President Marcos. One factor is the widespread cheating that happened during the snap election. Another factor is the support of the Catholic Church. This was through Jaime Cardinal Sin's radio message. Another factor is the discontent with how the country is being run by Marcos and his cronies.

In this paragraph, the sentences are grammatically correct and the ideas actually flow from one sentence to another. However, you will notice that each sentence is a simple sentence that contains just one subject and one predicate. Although there is nothing wrong with having simple sentences, sentences that do not transition smoothly can seem choppy and disconnected. When writing a paragraph where sentences are not connected, it will seem as if each sentence can stand as its own idea, and that the paragraph does not convey just one thought.

One way of addressing this is by using **transition expressions** that help connect ideas from one sentence to the other. There are different transition words that give an effect or show the relationship between the previous and current sentences or ideas. Learning when to use the correct transition word is important to help clarify the connection between your ideas. Below are categories of transitional expressions that may help in connecting sentences:

- **Cause and Effect:** *accordingly, because of, consequently, due to, hence, henceforth, owing to, therefore,* and *thus.*
- **Concession:** *admittedly, at any rate, despite this, in spite of, naturally, of course, regardless, while,* and *without a doubt.*
- **Condition:** *as long as, even if, granting that, if... then, in the event that, provided that, unless, when,* and *whenever.*
- **Contrast:** *although, but, contrary, conversely, even though, except, however, nevertheless, on the contrary,* and *on the other hand.*
- **Emphasis or Addition:** *above and beyond, additionally, again, also, alternatively, apart from, as a matter of fact, besides, following this, further, in addition, incidentally, likewise,* and *moreover.*
- **Sequence:** *first/second/third, a/b/c, after that, until, next, then,* and *finally.*
- **Time and Place:** *as, in, since, until, when, where,* and *while.*[73]

These words help bridge ideas between sentences or within sentences. When used correctly, they show how two sentences are connected to each other, and they signal the relationship between these sentences. These expressions can show whether you are adding an idea or refuting a previous statement, showing causation or highlighting the sequence. When used improperly or when used too much, these transitional expressions can confuse your readers about the relationships of your sentences. An overload of transition actually reduces, rather than aids, readability. Thus, transitions should be used strategically to show the relationship between sentences. Some examples of transitional expressions are:

> *Although* there were many factors behind the EDSA People Power Revolution, scholars argue that the main factor is the blatant cheating during the snap election.
> *However,* there are also opinions that people would not have joined if not for the support of the Catholic Church.
> *In addition to* the support of the Church, the later involvement of the military has also influenced the success of the revolution.

In these examples, we see how transitional expressions can show how different ideas are related to each other. The third sentence is particularly noteworthy since it also introduces another way of creating smooth transitions between sentences. This technique comes when you link the beginning of the sentence to the end of the previous sentence. In the example, the end of the previous sentence (Catholic Church) was used in the beginning part of the next sentence. This helps readers see how the new information connects with the old information.[74]

A variation of this technique is by using "this" or "it" (or "these" for plural ideas) to refer to something from the previous sentence. When using this technique, it is best not to make readers figure out what *this* or *these* means; it is best to just spell it out. For example,

> Significant changes came after the People Power Revolution.
> *Incorrect:* **These** included the drafting of a new constitution, the restoration of....
> *Correct:* **These changes** included the drafting of...

In the correct example, you clarified what the word "these" was referring to in the previous sentence. It thus becomes a way of connecting the two sentences through a singular idea.

A third way of ensuring the smooth transitions between sentences is to make **parallel structures**, which happens when two pieces of information are deliberately given similar forms. Parallel structures can be present between words and phrases (e.g. "I love hiking, running, swimming, and biking" not "I love hiking, running, to swim, and to bike") and they provide a way for organizing the sentences that come after it. For example, if you say that hiking, running, swimming, and biking are easy-to-do exercises, your next four sentences may talk about each one in turn—without the need for transitional expressions.[75]

Similar to how sentences can at times seem disconnected from each other, paragraphs can also be disconnected and will need to flow as well. This is a little more difficult to do since the "**idea chunks**" are much larger than sentences. When working with connecting paragraphs, it will be best to outline the broad ideas for each paragraph and how these ideas flow from one to another. First, you should clarify the point of every paragraph and see if there is a unity of ideas in that paragraph. Remember that one paragraph should just be limited to one main idea. Second, try to read the first sentence or sentences of every paragraph and see if the ideas flow between the paragraphs. It will be important to note how your ideas progress from one paragraph to the next. Third, and if necessary, change the order of paragraphs so that the progression of ideas is clearer.

By using transitional expressions, linking old and new information, ensuring parallel structures, and ordering the progression of ideas, you ensure that your readers will be able to read your sentences and paragraphs clearly. However, you must remember that using too many of these can actually confuse your reader. Thus, the effective use of these techniques should aid, not lessen, the paper's readability.

5.4 Mistakes in sentence construction

Research and academic papers usually start as assignments in senior high school or college, and the focus is on the content of the research rather than the usage of the language. However, there are times when beginning researchers forget important grammatical rules or are not prepared enough to recognize grammatical mistakes. Thus, the book also talks about common sentence mistakes in research, which even seasoned researchers could fall into:

- Subject-verb agreement errors
- Incorrect tense
- Sentence fragments
- Incorrect sentence structures
- Long sentences

One of the basic rules of the English language is that a singular subject takes a singular verb while a plural subject takes a plural verb. This means that (1) there should be both a subject and a verb in a sentence, and (2) you have to identify (almost naturally) what the subject and verbs are in the sentence. One mistake is that the subject and the verb are so far apart that it is hard to identify them in the sentence:

The policy that banned trucks from entering certain roads in Metro Manila, Cebu, and Davao have been implemented.

In the example, it is easy to mistake "trucks," "roads," or "Metro Manila, Cebu, and Davao" as the subjects of the sentence. But when one reads it thoroughly, the subject is "policy." This, however, is difficult to see since the subject and the verb are too far apart. Thus, one principle in writing sentences is to **keep the subject and verb close** to each other.[76] Some other subject-verb agreement mistakes can arise as you write your research:

(1) One of the authors like to write fantasy films.
(2) There is many implications to the new research.

In the first example, it is easy to think that the subject is "authors" but the subject is actually "one," which means that the verb should take on the singular form ("likes"). Thus, one has to be careful with **identifying the subject**, rather than just the noun closest to the verb.

For the second sentence, you will sometimes find yourself starting the sentence with "there" and the verb often used is the singular form. However, there are times when the subject is actually plural in form (e.g. "implications"), and so the verb prior to this word should take the plural form. This is a little tricky since we usually experience verbs coming after subjects but in this example, the order is different.

Another mistake when it comes to research is the **incorrect tense** for the verb. How do you know when to use the past, present, and future tenses? Particularly in research, there are times when tenses have to change depending on what you are referring to, and there are research conventions on when to use what type of language. In the following examples, think of what the correct verb should be:

The average human (walks, walked) 30 kilometers every month.
In one experiment, the average participant (walks, walked) 40 kilometers.

For the first sentence, the correct verb is the **present tense** "walks" because the idea is being stated as a matter of fact. For the second sentence, the correct verb is the **past tense** "walked" because there was an event that transpired or was completed (that is, the experiment). Thus, when writing research, you have to distinguish between statements of facts and situations that are always true (which take the present tense) and statements of events, experiments, or completed studies (which take the past tense).[77] In terms of sections, there are also common tenses that are used:

- **Introduction** and **literature review**: Present tense is used to describe authors' *point of view* while past tense is used to describe the *completed study*. (e.g. Many researchers argue that... One study conducted an experiment with...)
- **Methods** and **results**: Often, the simple past tense is used to highlight *action completed* (e.g. One key informant said...). However, when you refer to *figures*, *tables*, or *graphs*, you should use the present tense (e.g. Table 1 shows the...).
- **Discussion:** As with the introduction section, you must use the past tense to describe what was *completed* or *observed* and the present tense to describe the *significance*, *interpretation*, or *explanation* (e.g. Patterns were observed in weather changes in the past 20 years... They show that...).[78]

As a general rule, the **future tense** is not used in research, unless you are suggesting that you will have a follow-up experiment or something that will come at a future time. Unlike with other papers where students are asked to be consistent with the tense, research papers will need different tenses at different points. The above rules hope to provide you with ideas on the preferred tense to use, and it will be good to expose yourself to other studies and how other researchers write their papers.

Aside from problems with subject-verb agreement and verb tenses, another mistake committed is when these "sentences" lack a subject, a verb, or both. This is often called **sentence fragments**, when there are incomplete sentences that do not have an independent clause. Take, for example, "He wanted to make a point. To prove he was right." The first sentence is a complete one because there is clearly a subject and a verb. However, the second sentence seems to be part of the previous one as it starts with the verb "to prove." When faced with this problem, you may either supply the missing subject or verb, or combine sentences to complete the thought.

Another set of mistakes when writing research is incorrect sentence structures: misplaced or dangling modifier and sentence run-ons. A **misplaced modifier** is a word or phrase that is separated from the word it modifies while a **dangling modifier** is a word or phrase that modifies a word not clearly stated in the sentence. Unlike a misplaced modifier, a dangling modifier cannot be solved simply by changing the word order. When you commit these mistakes, sentences can sound weird or ridiculous. Here are some examples and how they can be corrected:

> *Incorrect:* Writing their research, the teacher helped her students.
> *Correct:* The teacher helped her students writing their research.
> *Incorrect:* Reading on the topic, the internet is a recent innovation.
> *Correct:* Reading on the topic, he learned that the internet is a recent innovation.

One way of addressing this is by identifying the modifier and seeing if it describes the correct word. In the first example, "writing their research" should be identified with the students but is written before the word "teacher." In the second example, the internet cannot do any "reading on the topic" so you will have to clarify what the modified noun is. When you have a case of a misplaced modifier, look for the word the modifier identifies and place it closer to that word. For dangling modifiers, you will have to supply the missing word since it is not present in the current sentence.

Connected to misplaced and dangling modifiers are **run-on sentences** that happen when two main clauses are connected without any punctuation. For example, "The writers were cooking the readers were eating." is clearly a run-on sentence since it seems as if the writers were cooking the readers—which is not a pretty picture. To address run-on sentences, you have to put in the correct punctuation mark, whether a comma or a semi-colon, or use conjunctives, such as *while* or *and*. But beware of the comma splice, in which a comma is used to connect two clauses when a semi-colon or even a period would do a better job.

Another consideration for your research is the sentence length and variety. A good way of avoiding monotony in your research writing is by **varying the length and structure** of your sentences—that is, having a mixture of short, medium, and long sentences, or a mixture of simple, complex, and compound sentences. One thing you have to be very careful with is when long sentences become confusing and difficult to read. Some things to remember when writing these longer or more complex sentences:

- Focus on your message. Each sentence should have a singular idea, no matter the length or the structure of the sentence.
- When your sentence is too long (maybe 50 words already), try to remove conjunctions and separate them into two sentences. This will help your readers know which ideas to focus on.
- Identify your subject and verb and keep them close to each other. A long and complex sentence is alright if you can clearly identify these two main parts (that is, subject and verb), and organize the structure strategically.
- Remember that a complex sentence has a subordinate clause (dependent on the main part, thought, or clause of the sentence) while a compound sentence joins two or more independent clauses.

Sentence mistakes are not as big a concern as plagiarism or wrong tables, but there are readers who can be put off by these small mistakes. By being accurate with the details of your sentences, you are helping your readers focus more on the content of your research rather than the style—and this focus will go a long way.

5.5 Mistakes with words

Aside from sentences, there are also a number of mistakes that can come with the wrong usage of words.

You should avoid **informal language** or spellings. Using tonite, thru, and tho are wrong for academic writing. One should also use clothes instead of *threads*, criminals instead of *crooks*, alcohol instead of *booze* since there is a preference for formal spelling.[79]

There are also some common practices that should be avoided. First, avoid using **contractions** like *can't, should've, I've* because of their informality. Second, avoid **abbreviations** like *decaf, etc., tbsp.* since some people may not be familiar with what these abbreviations mean. Lastly, avoid using **acronyms** if they have not yet been defined. When using acronyms like the AA, the acronym should first be defined as "Alcoholics Anonymous (AA)" or "Assumption Antipolo (AA)" during the first time it is used. These principles ensure that you help your readers who may not be familiar with certain contractions, abbreviations, and acronyms.

In terms of phrases, there are some that can be reduced to single words. You must prefer **concise writing** to wordy writing:

Wordy writing	**Concise writing**
a number of	many
a small number of	a few
are in agreement	agree
at present	now
prior to	before
subsequent to	after
based on the fact that	because
despite the fact that	although
if it is assumed that	if
in consequence of this	therefore/ consequently[80]
advance planning	planning
an unexpected surprise	a surprise
ask a question	ask
basic fundamentals	fundamentals
completely empty	empty
in order to	to
in spite of the fact that	although/ despite
new innovation	innovation
past history	history

repeat again	repeat
two different kinds	two kinds
very unique	unique[81]

Aside from wordy phrases, you should also be careful with words that are often **mistakenly interchanged**:

- In common usage, **affect** is a verb that means to influence or make a difference to, and **effect** is usually a noun that means the result of a change. However, affect is sometimes used as a noun to refer to "emotions" while effect can be a verb. As an example of the first or more common usage, you can *affect* the decision and its *effect* may be significant.
- **Advice** is a noun used to refer to a recommendation that was given while **advise** is a verb when someone recommends something. For example, the coach *advised* his players to strengthen the defense, and the team felt that this was sound *advice*.
- **Complement** means an addition that improves on something while a **compliment** is a praise or an expression of approval. For example, the dinner guest *complimented* the chef and remarked that the side dish was a wonderful *complement* to the steak.
- **Their** is the possessive case of the pronoun "they" while **there** is an adverb that means in that place. For example, *their* books are over *there.*
- **Then** denotes time or doing something next in a series while **than** denotes the comparison of two things. Thus, you can say that a girl received a gift that was better *than* she deserved, so *then* she felt guilty.

When writing numbers, according to the American Psychological Association, use **words** for numbers below 10 (zero to nine) and **numerals** for numbers 10 and above. Lastly, when using jargon or technical terms, be sure to provide a definition or description when the term is first used in the research.

You may also try **diversifying the words** you use when these words recur a lot in your research. For example, the term *research* can repeat a lot, when you can use words like "paper," "investigation," "study," or "research project." The term *analyze* can also occur frequently, and you can opt for other words like "examine," "investigate," "explore," "scrutinize," or "observe."

You have to be careful, however, that you do not overdo this for **technical words** that have specific meanings. It will be best that your readers are not confused about how particular words are used for your research. For example, "achievement" and "attainment" may seem similar but education research differentiates the two, so you will have to make that distinction early on. It will also be best to be accurate about the words you write. For example, will your research distinguish between "learning" and "education"? Again, although they can be used as synonyms, do you plan to use one in a particular situation and the other for another situation? Such considerations will matter if you hope your readers to clearly follow your research.

5.6 Mistakes with italics, bold, and underline

Sometimes it is fascinating how some students would underline and put in bold and italics a word in order to give it emphasis. However, when emphasizing a word, it is enough to choose just one: *italics* are for light emphasis, **bold** faces are for heavy emphasis, while underlines are for handwritten papers. In most research papers, the most common tool for emphasis is putting words in italics. For textbooks with a lot of information and key words (like the one you are holding), it is best to emphasize with a bold face so that the words and ideas can be easily distinguished.

Italics, in particular, have other uses in research. You should put in italics titles, foreign words or phrases, words as linguistic examples, scientific names, and statistics. Here are some examples:

Book title: *Pride and Prejudice* is an example of....
Journal title: The *Philippine Sociological Review* publishes...
Cinema: The movie *One More Chance* starred....
Television or radio programs: One of the longest-running shows is *Eat Bulaga!*
Artwork: Fernando Zobel's *Carroza* is an iconic...

Some titles that do not need to be italicized are sacred texts like the Koran or the Bible, or even the books in the Bible (e.g. Genesis,

Mark, Revelations). In addition, when faced with shorter works such as book chapters and journal articles, these should be **inside quotation marks** and not in italics. For example, you can write about a chapter on "The Market and the Polis" that came from the book *Policy Paradox: The Art of Political Decision Making*, or an article on "What high-achieving low-income students know about college" found in the journal *American Economic Review*.

Other examples for italics include:

Foreign words: *Eid'l Fitr* is celebrated in the Philippines... (However, foreign words that have become part of the English language need not be in italics, like etc., bon voyage, or bona fide.)
Words as linguistic examples: The word *cosmopolitan* comes from the...
Scientific names: The type of bee used was *Apis mellifera lamarckii* or Egyptian honey bee...
Statistics: The sample is relatively old (M = 57.33, SD = 3.62). [M stands for the mean and SD for the standard deviation. Other statistical notations in italics include t, F, p, R^2, r, and β]

Aside from italics, one should also be careful with **capitalizations** when emphasizing ideas. There have been a couple of incidences when some students or researchers would put their ideas in ALL CAPS to show emphasis. This might work with text messages but not with formal research papers.

5.7 Mistakes in punctuation

In grade school, one is taught that you use a period (.) to end a declarative sentence and you use a comma (,) to separate ideas. As students progress in school, they learn other punctuation marks, and there are times when people forget the preferred use for a particular punctuation mark. Here is a refresher on when to use certain punctuations:

- **Semicolon (;)** – You use a semicolon when you are *joining two complete ideas* without a conjunction. For example, "The basketball team had many missed shots; this resulted in a lost game."

You should also use a semicolon when your *list already has commas*. For example, "The writers include Jackie, a graduate from UP; Jason, a graduate from NUS; and Oscar, a professor from Yale."

- **Colon (:)** – There are at least three ways of using a colon: when *introducing a list* (e.g. The experiment happened in three places: Manila, Singapore, and New York.); when *showing emphasis* (e.g. There was only one option after the storm: move to another city.); or when *introducing a quote* (e.g. He had one reply: "I don't know.").
- **Hyphen (-)** – Use a hyphen when *connecting two or more words*, e.g. brother-in-law, sugar-free, bad-tempered, up-to-date, and camera-ready.
- **Dash (—)** – There are two types of dash: an **n-dash** is a little longer than a hyphen and is usually used for *dates* (e.g. 1921 – 1931) while an **m-dash** is longer than an n-dash and is often used to create a *break in the structure* of the sentence (e.g. Da Vinci's drawings—often thought ahead of its time—have been studied by researchers…).
- **Parentheses ( )** – These are often used for *added* or *clarificatory information*. They can also be used to *enclose numbers* or letters, e.g. The men included (1) Jose Rizal, (2) Andres Bonifacio….
- **Quotation marks (" ")** – In research, this is often used when *repeating what someone else said or wrote verbatim*, when *referring to a word, phrase or slang* (e.g. "Bagets" is a common slang for teen-agers."), or when *using titles for articles, chapters, poems, etc.* (e.g. "Desiderata" is a 1927 poem…)
- **Apostrophe (')** – This is often used to *show possession* or to *mark the omission of a letter* (as in a contraction).[82]

Mistakes in punctuation can come in many forms, like not putting a period at the end of a sentence, substituting a semicolon for a colon, using quotation marks instead of parentheses, and so on. With the above clarification, one hopes to reduce these mistakes.

5.8 Mistakes in footnote citations

When writing your research, it is important to properly cite where you got information so that readers and other researchers may be able to ascertain your facts or provide them other leads if they plan to do research themselves. There are different ways of citing sources. In this section, I talk about the common mistakes that come with using the Chicago Manual of Style's **notes citation.**

Notes can be used either as footnotes at the bottom of the page or as endnotes at the end of the whole document. Usually, the notes will include important information such as the authors' full name, journal article/ chapter title, book/ journal title, volume, place of publication, publisher, date of publication, and the page number. When using the Chicago Manual of Style, there is also a pattern for doing it in the notes section:

[1] Author's first name and last name, "Book Chapter Title [if any]," **in** *Book Title in Italics* **(**Place of Publication**:** Publisher**,** Year of Publication**),** Page Number/s.

[2] Author's first name and last name, "Journal Article Title," *Journal Title* Volume**, no.** Issue **(**Year**):** Page Number/s.

There are many other variations for this, and one may refer to the book *The Chicago Manual of Style 17th Edition* or to *Researching Philippine Realities* for more details.[83] For now, we talk about the common mistakes when using the notes citation:

- When writing notes, some make the mistake of using **both footnotes and endnotes**. However, you will have to clarify your choice and consistently use it in your research. Using footnotes is helpful if you want your readers to *immediately know* where you obtained information (particularly useful for disciplines such as history and law). On the other hand, using endnotes is helpful to *improve the readability* so that readers are not distracted by notes at the bottom of the page.
- Another common mistake is to **make the wrong indention**. For footnotes and endnotes, you should have a *paragraph indent*, where the first line starts 0.5 inches from the left margin while the subsequent lines follow the left margin. This is different when you write the references section since you will have to use *hanging indent*, where the first line starts at the

left margin while the subsequent lines are indented 0.5 inches from the left margin.

- A third mistake happens with the **author's name placement.** Often the mistake happens when the author's family name comes first in the notes section. When writing the notes, you have to write the author's *first name before the family name*. But when writing the references, you should write the family name first so that the references can be alphabetically arranged by family name.
- Another mistake comes with the **proper marks for titles**. Sometimes, students get confused about when to use *quotation marks* and *italics*. It must be noted that book chapters and journal articles should be inside quotation marks while book and journal titles should be in italics. One must also note to *capitalize the beginning letter* of important words and not capitalize the whole title.
- When writing the **publication details** for books, researchers may mistake the order of details. It must start with the *city of publication* (e.g. Manila, Los Angeles) followed by a colon, and then followed by the *publisher's name*. After this, there should be a comma followed by the *year of publication*.
- For **journal details**, you must include the *volume* and the *issue* number, followed by the *year* it was published inside parentheses.
- When referring to the **entry immediately before**, you need not write the whole citation again. It is perfectly fine to write "Ibid., [page number]." This word signals that the reader should refer to the previous citation.
- When referring to an **entry that has been cited** but not immediately before, you again do not need to write the whole citation. You only need to write the author's *last name*, shortened *book title* or *journal article title*, and the *page* you are referring to.
- Lastly, mistakes come when the footnoted citations do not appear on the **references section** of the research as bibliographic entries.

You may also use **citation management systems** like Zotero, Mendeley, or EndNote. (A guide for using Zotero is found in the book *Researching Philippine Realities.*) When using these, you still have to be careful about mistakes that can arise from inaccurate citations that have been automatically generated. These citation systems are there to help, but nothing beats knowing how to spot citation mistakes.

5.9 Mistakes with in-text citations

Aside from footnote citations used often in the humanities and business fields, the Chicago Manual of Style also uses in-text citations (also known as the **author-date style**). Rather than talk about the reference at the bottom of the page, the citation is shown with the author/s' last name/s and the year when the research or book was published. In order to see the full detail of the research, you may refer to the works cited or references section, which provides details similar to the footnotes. This in-text citation format is also used by the American Psychological Association—preferred in the social sciences.

Here are various ways of writing in-text citations for the Chicago Manual of Style:

> Teachers can feel resistance to technology… (Howard 2013).
> It was mentioned that, "Teaching with technology…" (Koehler and Mishra 2009, 61).
> Lim (2007) highlights implications for the integration….

In the first example, the sentence immediately prior to the reference in parentheses should refer to the idea you are using from your reference. Thus, the paraphrased or summarized idea from Howard's research connected to the present research is mentioned in this sentence. If you quote a line from the research (similar to the second example), you should put it inside quotation marks and write the page number in addition to the authors' last names and year of publication. If you plan to mention the authors' names in the paragraph, you only need to write the year of publication within parentheses immediately after the authors' name.

When you use the citation style for the American Psychological Association, the only difference is the comma separating the family name and the year of publication. Thus, it is formatted as (Howard, 2013) and (Koehler and Mishra, 2009, p. 61).

Despite the seeming simplicity, there are still mistakes committed when writing these in-text citations:

- Sometimes when people quote a line from the research, they forget to write the **page number** where they got the information. Putting the page number is important, however, so that readers will know what page to refer to if they want to get more information about the research.
- If there are **more than two authors**, there are different sets of rules that guide them. The common mistake is to mention all the authors' family names. However, the rule is to have all the names only for those with up to **three authors**. For those that have four or more authors, you only need to write the first author's last name and include "et al." after it. An example of this is (Veldman et al. 2016).
- Another mistake is to mention the author's name on the paragraph but **fail to include the year published** immediately after the name. It is important to also write the year of publication since authors usually have more than one published work, and when you are referring to it in the references, you need to show which one you are referring to.
- Similarly, there are times when you refer to **two published works** of the same author, published in the **same year**. During these times, it is best to write the year with a letter after it to distinguish one published work from another. For example, Dr. Jayeel Cornelio had at least two published papers in 2016, and so, the citation will be written as (Cornelio 2016a) and (Cornelio 2016b).

For the **works cited** or **reference** section, there is a usual format that includes details similar to the notes citation. This is usually called the bibliography of most research. Examples include:

Chicago Manual of Style (CMS) bibliography:

Howard, Sarah K. 2013. "Risk-Aversion: Understanding Teachers' Resistance to Technology Integration." *Technology, Pedagogy and Education* 22 (3): 357–72.

Koehler, Matthew, and Punya Mishra. 2009. "What Is Technological Pedagogical Content Knowledge (TPACK)?" *Contemporary Issues in Technology and Teacher Education* 9 (1): 60–70.

Lim, Cher Ping. 2007. "Effective Integration of ICT in Singapore Schools: Pedagogical and Policy Implications." *Educational Technology Research and Development* 55 (1): 83–116.

Boud, David, and Grahame Feletti. 1997. *The Challenge of Problem-Based Learning*. London: Kogan Page.

American Psychological Association (APA) bibliography:

Howard, S. K. (2013). Risk-aversion: understanding teachers' resistance to technology integration. *Technology, Pedagogy and Education*, 22(3), 357–372.

Koehler, M., & Mishra, P. (2009). What is Technological Pedagogical Content Knowledge (TPACK)? *Contemporary Issues in Technology and Teacher Education*, 9(1), 60–70.

Lim, C. P. (2007). Effective integration of ICT in Singapore schools: pedagogical and policy implications. *Educational Technology Research and Development*, 55(1), 83–116.

Boud, D., & Feletti, G. (1997). *The Challenge of Problem-based Learning*. London: Kogan Page.

In both cases, the bibliography should include the references **alphabetically arranged** with the author's last name. For CMS, the first name should be spelled out while for APA, only the initials are necessary. The year is also written immediately after with the authors' names though for CMS, the year is not written inside parentheses while for APA, it is written inside them. Similar to notes citations, the journal or book title should be in italics and the journal article or book chapter should just be within quotation marks for CMS and no marks for APA. Common mistakes for the reference section include:

- entries not arranged alphabetically;
- wrong use of names, e.g. initials for CMS and full names for APA;
- non-italicized titles; and
- incomplete details in terms of city and publisher, or volume and issue number.

Writing citations—and remembering the proper format for its writing—is often difficult and involves a lot of details. Nonetheless, this is a crucial part of research writing and knowing its principles will help in future work that involve numerous details.

CHAPTER 6
MISTAKES IN PUBLICATION

Many beginning researchers think that once they are done with the research writing, they are done with the research. When you submit your research to your thesis committee or your organization, that is usually the end of the research line. However, after you conducted your research and wrote about it, you can take it a step further by having it published as a book chapter, a journal article, or a personal entry for your academic website, such as ResearchGate or Academia.

To publish your research is to make it public, to share your findings to a broader community with the aim that some other person may benefit from the insights or topics you have written about. You can argue that one of the biggest mistakes for any researcher is to keep the research to oneself—without other people knowing about the methods you have used or the information you have collected. When you do research and share it, you are not just fulfilling an intellectual curiosity; you are also helping expand the knowledge base and organize the understanding of a topic.

As with the other parts of the research process, there are still some mistakes that can come in the publication process. It may be about submitting to the wrong journal and not disclosing conflicts of interest, or about disregarding the comments of your paper's reviewers. In this short chapter, I hope that you will be able to have an insider's knowledge of the publication process to assist you when sending in your paper for publication.

Although not all people will necessarily want to publish their research, I hope to encourage you to at least consider and try sending your research for publication in a journal. Having a published article will be helpful if you plan to land an academic job as a professor, or if you want to gain more credibility in your profession. Another benefit of publishing your research is for the institution you are part of. Most journal articles show your institutional or university affiliation, and your published article helps the standing and reputation of your institution. More than the personal and institutional benefits of having a published research, there are also social benefits if your research carries practical or conceptual significance.

If your research is necessary knowledge for further knowledge to be created, your choice not to share your research to the wider community will actually be a disservice to others. Thus, this chapter shares common mistakes when writing this section so that you do not commit them.

6.1 Submitting to the wrong journal

If you have been convinced that there are merits to your submitting your research to an academic journal, you will likely have to find a journal that your research should be in. You can think of **academic and scientific journals** as specialized books published every quarter (or semi-annually or annually) that show new discoveries in the journal's specialization. There are broad journals like *Science* and *Cell* where articles span different disciplines while there are also very specialized journals where articles concentrate on a very specific interdisciplinary field or subdiscipline, such as biostatistics, or the educational use of artificial intelligence. When you submit to a journal, it will typically go through a review process where your papers will be sent anonymously to "reviewers" for their comments, suggestions, and decision (whether to reject, accept, or revise).

One crucial mistake is to submit to the wrong journal by not taking time to **assess the fit** between your research findings and the journal's aims and scope. Most journals will have webpages that detail the types of research they accept, the fields they focus on, the aims of the accepted research papers, and how narrowly or broadly they accept certain papers. It is best to know as much about the journal as possible and assess if your paper fits the journals' aims and scope. Choosing the wrong journal can actually heighten the risk of your paper's rejection because the paper does not match the focus of the journal.

Aside from going to the journal's homepage and seeing if the aims and scope match your research, you may also look at your own **bibliography** and see where your cited materials come from. Are there journals that you continually cite? Are there journals in your bibliography that connect well with your research? Are there journals that have similar titles as your research? Going through your bibliography can help you see which journals will likely accept a paper similar to yours, and so it is a good place to start.

Another place to start when looking for the right journal to publish in is going to the Internet and using **search engines** to look for journals in your particular field or area. You can go to Google Scholar, Scopus, or Elsevier Journal Finder to see which journals publish the type of research you conducted. When going through the journals, you may want to take note of some details about them:

- **Impact factor** shows the average number of citations the journal's articles have had in the past two years. The impact factor can be a proxy for the journal's reputation and a high impact factor generally shows that many researchers trust the journal and cite its articles.
- **Review speed** highlights how long the average review period is. This is particularly helpful if you want to know how long, on average, it will take for your paper to be reviewed.
- **Acceptance rate** displays the percentage of papers that are accepted by the journal. A low acceptance rate means that the journal may be highly selective in the papers they approve for publication.
- **Instructions for authors** show the various writing conventions for the journal. It may include the citation style, the acceptable languages (English, Spanish, etc.), and the word limit.
- **Readership** highlights the type of reader the journal has.

When looking for the right journal for your research paper, there are many things to keep in mind in terms of the fit between your paper and the journal's aims. If one goes back to the word "publishing" (which means to make public), one of the most important criteria would be which journal will your intended reader be reading. It is often a good practice to imagine the readers you want (e.g. practitioners, doctors, academics, professors, and policy makers), and see which journals they likely read. When you know this, you will have a good gauge of which journal to submit to.[84]

The other thing you have to consider is how ready your research is for publication. Although you may have done your research well and you think you have something significant to share to a broader audience, you will have to assess if you research is **publishable.** Some questions you can ask yourself are:

- What is something new you are saying with your research?
- How have you shown what others have said about this topic?
- Why is this research significant enough for others to read?
- How does your research connect to all other studies made on this topic or in this discipline?

If you are unable to answer these questions with clarity, you may have to continue improving your manuscript before you submit it for review.

If you think your research is ready and you have found a journal that is a good fit, you will have to submit your manuscript. Some journals will ask you to upload your submission in a manuscript submission portal while other journals will ask you to email your submission directly to the editor or the journal's email handle. Again, these details will usually be clear in the journal's homepage.

An alternative to publishing your research in journals is presenting it in **academic conferences**. By participating in conferences, you get to make public your research and you also get insights on how to improve it. Questions and suggestions from conference participants can help you fine-tune your research so that you can have a stronger submission to a journal.

6.2 Submitting to two journals at a time

Some researchers think that submitting to two or more journals increases the chances of their paper being accepted by at least one journal. However, this is one of the cardinal mistakes in journal submissions. You should not submit your journal to **more than one journal** at a single time. If your paper is rejected by one journal, you may submit to a different journal but your paper should not be under the review or publication process in two journals at the same time. The only solution to this mistake is to not submit your paper to more than one journal.

You may be asking why on earth you have to limit your submission to just one journal at a time. There are two reasons for this. The first reason is because of the **time wasted** if you submit your paper to two or more journals. Journal editors have the difficult task of looking for reviewers to see if your paper is fit for publication. When a submission is already accepted in one journal, the time spent by the reviewers and editors in the other journal will have been wasted if the submission will be withdrawn by the author. Additionally, the reviewer might find out that he or she has to review the same paper from two different journals, which will signal that the research is in the review process for at least two journals.

The second reason not to submit to more than one journal is because of the possibility of the journal articles being **published by both journals** that had accepted the research paper. For one article to be published in a journal means that the journal has the exclusive rights to that paper's publication. However, when a research paper is published in two journals (and they do not acknowledge each other), this can signal a clear conflict of interest. Redundant publications can adversely affect meta-studies that overstate the effect of a particular phenomenon simply because it has been published in more than one journal.[85]

This is the reason why your **cover letter** should usually include a sentence that says, "I/ We confirm that this work is original and has not been published elsewhere, nor is it currently under consideration for publication elsewhere." A cover letter (which will be described in greater depth later) is a letter to the editor detailing the merits of your research and requesting that the paper be considered for review. An explicit indication that the paper has not been submitted to another journal is important to highlight that you are only having this considered by the journal you are submitting to.

6.3 Absent or unclear abstracts

When you look at scientific publications, it is not unusual for these papers to have more than 40 references. If there are more than 40 references, there is a high chance that the author must have read through or skimmed even more than that number. When you write your research paper, you will have to sift through copious information, and it will be very difficult—if not, impossible—to read comprehensively all the papers on your topic. This is why abstracts are so important because they give a summary of the research and tells you whether the article will be helpful for your research purposes.

Among the more common mistakes of beginning researchers is to forget writing the abstract or have an unclear view of what should be written in the abstract. Since most journals will ask you to submit an abstract together with your main research, it is best for you to know what exactly should be written in it. A **typical abstract** for a journal submission must usually answer these questions:

- What is your main research question?
- What is the motivation for this research question?/ Why is this significant?
- How did you go about answering that question?
- What are your main findings or arguments?
- [If there is still space,] What do these findings mean broadly?[86]

The difficult part about the abstract is that you must **condense** your whole research to a paragraph of just **150 to 250 words**. The word limits are varied for different journals, so it is best to check how many words are usually allotted for the abstracts in a journal. Some journals also have a **more structured** format, where each section is spelled out. For example, journals in Emerald Insight usually have these sections:

- **Purpose** talks about the primary motivation for the study, inclusive of the main research question.
- **Design/methodology/approach** highlights how the research was conducted, who were the participants, what methods were used for data collection and data analysis.
- **Findings** section displays the significant results and new insights from the research.
- **Research limitations** section shows the shortcomings or conditions that the researcher cannot control.
- **Practical implication** provides how the research insights can be used or applied to everyday life.
- **Originality/value** focuses on what novel ideas were uncovered in the course of the research.

When writing a more structured abstract, you should write the bullet (e.g. Findings) and then follow it with one to three sentences describing the summary of what is referred to. When writing an unstructured abstract, you have the freedom to move things around in the same paragraph. You just have to remember that your abstract should provide your readers an overview of your research and a pitch for what is unique about it.

Think of your abstract as a way for you to **sell your idea** (not that you will be richer from selling it). You have to show your readers what you have done and why it is important for them to continue reading. The abstract is a place for you to entice your reader about the importance of your research and the consequences of your findings. Just be careful though that you do not sound like an overly enthusiastic salesperson more interested in making a pitch than sharing an idea. If your research is good and your abstract is clear, this will be more than enough to entice your reader.

6.4 Weak cover letter

When I started writing research, I thought writing the abstract was the final part and I could just send it over to the journal editors.

However, there are times when you have to write a cover letter that introduces your research submission to the editors. Think of it as a letter that details **why the journal should publish** your paper. One mistake that people make is failing to write a strong cover letter that provides justification for why the research paper merits publication. Here's one example of how not to write your letter:

> To whom it may concern:
>
> I am sending an interesting paper on our research.
> I really think that the paper is suitable for your journal.
> I hope you like it.
>
> Thanks so much,
> Jackie

A letter like that will definitely make the editors question if you are really serious about your journal submission.

A cover letter is a formal letter that includes the journal editor's full name, affiliation, and address (if necessary). You must make the effort to know who the current editor-in-chief is, so that you may correctly address the cover letter. Inside the cover letter's body, your first paragraph should include details of what you are submitting and an explicit statement that it is submitted solely to the journal.

The next paragraph should provide a short summary of what the research is about and how thoroughly you have done research on it. You do not need to rewrite the abstract in this section; you just need to give a bird's eye-view picture of the research. After this paragraph, you should provide a justification for why the research is suitable for publication in the journal. You should show how the research you made fits the journal's aims and scope, and how the journal's readers will benefit from the research you have written.[87]

The last paragraph should just state whether you have conflicts of interest that need to be disclosed, and your preferred means of correspondence for concerns with the manuscript. Below is an example of a fictional cover letter:

5 December 2019

Dr. Laurence Rivera
Editor, *Journal of Filipino Studies*

Dear Dr. Rivera,

I submit an original article entitled "Religiosity among Urban Poor Filipinos" for consideration by the *Journal of Filipino Studies*. I confirm that this work is original and has not been published elsewhere, nor is it currently under consideration for publication elsewhere.

In this paper, I show how urban poor Filipinos practice their religions and how religions affect their daily life. The paper highlights three themes in the practice of religion, which include…

I believe this paper is appropriate for publication in your journal because of the journal's focus on investigating different facets of Filipino life. The paper's focus on religion as experienced by Filipinos will shed greater light on….

Lastly, I have no conflicts of interest to disclose. If there are concerns, please address all correspondence to me at jhong@ignatius.edu.

Thank you very much for your consideration of this manuscript.

Sincerely,
Jackie Hong
Professor, Department of Sociology
Ignatius University

A cover letter can be written on the email message itself or it can be sent as an attachment. Some online submissions do not need a cover letter, so check the online submission if you are being asked for it.

6.5 Undisclosed conflicts of interest

There are times when a research is funded by an outside agency or when the results of a research could have monetary benefits for you, your institution, or your family member. During these times, these may be construed as conflicts of interest. These conflicts arise when the researcher's primary interest as a research may be at risk of being unduly influenced—or appear to be unduly influenced—by one's secondary interest, such as financial gain or personal advancement.[88]

These conflicts may come when financial or personal considerations may **compromise** or **appear to compromise** your judgment, conduct, and report of your research. It is important to remember that even if these considerations may not actually compromise your judgment, just the appearance of its compromising your judgment is already critical. If you are being paid by a political candidate to do a research on voters' perception of him, you will likely make an effort to be as faithful to your data as possible and not be swayed by your funder's personal graces. However, if you publish your research and not disclose this potential conflict of interest, this non-disclosure makes your research suspect.

On the one hand, disclosing is expected to increase transparency and trust between the researcher and the reader. On the other hand, disclosing may also lead the reader to an unconscious diminishment of confidence in the results of the research. This second effect of disclosure is natural because of how people may think that the research is influenced by the funders' aims. You may, of course, do your research with funding from independent agencies that will not provide any conflicts of interest. Whatever is your decision, you will have to identify and disclose when conflicts of interest arise.

6.6 Disregarding reviewer comments

If you submit your paper to an international journal, this will typically go through the **peer review process**, where independent reviewers—typically fellow researchers or professors in the field of the submitted manuscript—are invited to read your paper, comment on its fitness for publication, provide suggestions for its improvement, and help give information for journal editors to make an informed decision on whether to publish your submission. Typically, you will not know who the reviewers are, and at times, even the reviewers will not know who the author is.[89] The blind review ensures that the manuscript is judged from the merits of the research rather than from the seniority of the author.

This review process will usually take 3 to 6 months (depending on the journal and the number of submissions it processes), and there are five decision outcomes. **Desk rejection** happens when the editor or another member of the editorial board deems that your paper is not fit for review because of different issues: manuscript is not related to the scope of the journal, poor quality of writing, inaccurate methods, or other factors that could reduce the chances of the manuscript's getting through the review process. Although a desk rejection could be difficult for a researcher, one mistake is to treat this as a sign that your research is not worthy of publication. You can think of a desk rejection as something that will help you improve your submission, make you look for a truly suitable journal, and give you inspiration to focus on what needs to be done. You may also see this rejection positively since you were informed of the decision much earlier in the process.

Rejection with review comes when the editors send out your manuscript to reviewers because of some merits of your research but the reviewers found the paper lacking in some way, whether in the writing, design, analysis, or fitness. You must never think that a rejection by one journal's set of reviewers means that the research will be rejected automatically by another journal. Sometimes the issue is the fit more than the research analysis; sometimes the issue is the space for journal entries and not your research paper. Nonetheless, one temptation is to disregard the reviewers' comments and say that they do not understand your research. If this happens, be careful to ask yourself what comments have merit and need to be addressed before you submit to another journal. Having the humility to honestly assess your work will go a long way in advancing your academic career.

Revise and resubmit means that the reviewers and editors found some problems, flaws, and missing elements in your research, but they believe that with some changes, the paper may be publishable in the journal. When the editors relay this decision, they will usually include the reviewers' comments and suggestions on how to improve the manuscript. The editor will also likely provide some general direction for the changes that have to be made, particularly when reviewers provide conflicting advice. When you revise your submission, you will have to rewrite your manuscript and write a letter that addresses the comments of your reviewers. One of the cardinal mistakes made in this stage of the research is to disregard the reviewers' comments and not address them in your letter.

If you plan to revise your research, you have to first make changes in the original document. Sometimes, you will have to start over with your submission while at other times, you only need to track the changes that you have made. The editor will let you know if they prefer that you **highlight the changes** in the manuscript (or use the track changes function in Microsoft Word). If you do not agree with one of the reviewers' comments, you may decide not to include this particular change. However, you will have to **justify your decision** in the letter that details all the changes, improvements, and incorporated suggestions. It is best that you highlight how the present submission differs from the initial submission, and how the reviewers' comments have been addressed. Needless to say, your letter should be respectful despite your differences in opinions with your reviewers.

The last two types of decisions are **Accept with minor revisions** and **Accept without revisions**, which are extremely rare for first review—and even rarer for beginning researchers. This means that your article is already accepted pending the minor revisions that have to be made before it gets submitted to the layout artists. These are the decision letters that you hope will come after a successful revise and resubmit attempt.

6.7 Resting on your laurels

When you have a research published in a journal or accepted to a conference, you can think of that as a confirmation of your scholarly potential and the hard work you put for your research. You may even think of it as an award for the sacrifices you have made for your research. Yet one of the most tempting mistakes is to **rest and discontinue writing** after one publication. Since research is quite cognitively taxing and enervating, it is understandable to find solace in rest.

However, research is not like an award that you gain at the end of a published research project. Rather, research is like a sport that you continue to grow in. You need to continually train and improve yourself if you want to get ahead of the game. In a sense, after one publication, you will have to continue researching and publishing in order to push the boundaries of knowledge and contribute meaningfully to your field. You will have to network with different researchers to see how your projects are connected and maybe even to collaborate on projects with each other.

To rest on your laurels may be the biggest mistake when doing research. To say that you are done with research after one published article is a great disservice to the community who might benefit from the insights you have to share. Although research can be difficult and taxing, its **benefits to oneself** and **one's community** far outweigh any inconveniences. Its personal benefits to you include improving your thinking, satisfying your curiosity, and helping your decision-making. Its social benefits also have to be highlighted along with its effects on innovations, policies, medicine, art, and the whole knowledge enterprise.

It is my sincere wish that this book on research mistakes has helped **lighten the burden** of research by pointing out mistakes that can be easily avoided. By alerting you to some of these mistakes, I hope the book helps you find meaning in the research process and joy in its outcome.

RESEARCH PROCESS

	Mistakes	Remedies
1	Unclear purpose and audience	Clarify why you are writing the research (knowledge production, policy analysis, etc.). Keep in mind who you are writing for (general audience vs. specific experts in the field)
2	Procrastination	Try to manage your time well and chunk tasks. Be mindful of your scripts and delaying tactics. Create a matrix of activities in terms of urgency and importance.
3	Neglecting guidelines, rubrics, and instructions	Check the journal or department's instructions for writers, including spelling, word limit, citation style, and paper structure.
4	Infeasibility of research	Check ahead of time if you will be permitted by the institution, administrators, or officials to conduct your research. Discern if you have enough time to finish your research. Try doing pilot studies, surveys, or interviews with a smaller scale before going for a bigger scale.
5	Group conflicts	Manage each other's expectations and working styles from the start. Talk about how you plan to get feedback on your work. Beware of gift and ghost authorship.
6	Personal problems and emergencies	If there is a risk that a personal problem may occur during the conduct of your research, think in advance how you can address it. If the problem happens, tell your adviser or groupmates about your situation.

CONCEPTUALIZATION

	Mistakes	*Remedies*
1	Lack of preliminary reading	Read and reflect about the topic you wish to pursue. Get exposed to studies, both classic and recent.
2	Vague research questions	Be careful about having questions that are either too broad or too specific. Think of questions that are grounded in a particular reality or phenomenon. Avoid questions that are loaded with many assumptions. Be open to how your research question can change in the process of research.
3	Unidentified research gap	Think about how your research adds to our current knowledge or what new insights you plan to say. Avoid research topics that have been studied to death.
4	Unclear hypothesis or argument	Write a hypothesis that can be tested with the variables you have at your disposal. Write a tentative argument that clearly answers the research question.
5	Unaligned question and argument	You have the choice of either changing your argument or changing your research question.
6	Unclear research structure	Be familiar with the IMRAD model followed by most research in the natural, physical, and social sciences. Most research usually have sections on Introduction, Methods, Results, and Discussion.
7	Undefined terms	Write out acronyms during the first time they appear. Define scientific and technical terms during the first time they appear. Operationalize concepts such that they can be quantified or qualified.

8	Literature review as book or article summaries	Note that the literature review expresses your stance on a topic and need not be summaries of things you have read. Literature reviews can challenge previous research or provide a bird's eye-view of the topic.
9	Incoherent literature review	Create a structure for your literature review. This can take the form of topical arrangement, compare-and-contrast, advantages-and-disadvantages, chronological arrangement, factors, problem-and-solutions structure, etc.
10	Outdated or unreliable literature	Find up-to-date research, findings, and examples. Search in more reliable or scholarly search engines like Jstor, EBSCOHost, Google Books, Google Scholar, etc.
11	Unclear differentiation between framework and literature review	Although both help researchers conceptualize the study and identify research gaps, a literature review does not need a conceptual map but a framework should provide a structure of how ideas are connected with each other.

METHODS

	Mistakes	Remedies
1	Inappropriate research method	Clarify whether you will use a qualitative, quantitative, or mixed-methods approach. Think of a plan or strategy with how you will answer your research question. Reflect if the answer you obtain through your methods is the answer to your main research question.
2	Sampling mistakes	Distinguish whether you are doing probability or non-probability sampling. Be familiar with possible sources of bias with your data. Clarify what will make participants be included or excluded from your research.
3	Erroneous survey questionnaires	When creating your own tests, beware of common pitfalls and issues on confidentiality, inaccurate choices, different ranges, types of questions (and responses), using Likert scales, and having open- and closed-ended questions.
4	Interview and FGD mistakes	Use an interview when you want to get in-depth information or confidential narratives. Use FGDs when looking at social interactions and differences in perspectives. Provide information about your research to your participants. Give your participants time to prepare for the interview and send a formal invitation to let them know what will be asked of them. When doing the interview itself, have a coherent structure and come prepared with possible follow-up questions.
5	Untranscribed or uncoded data	Bring a recording device to record your informants' answers. Transcribe the interviews faithfully. Systematically code your interviews to see common themes and answers.
6	Unaddressed ethical concerns	If necessary, seek research ethics approval for your study. Clarify if you will be involving vulnerable populations in your research. Ensure confidentiality and privacy of your participants. Treat participants with respect and dignity.

7	Inability to foresee and disclose risks	Inform your research participants about the possible physical, psychological, social and, legal risks that come with joining the research (if there are any). Come prepared with plans to minimize the risk or how to address the problems when they happen.
8	Inability to obtain informed consent	Your letters to participants should include the purpose of your study, procedure and duration of involvement, potential risks and benefits, statement of voluntary participation and right to withdraw, ensuring confidentiality of data, asking permission for recording, compensation, and contact information.
9	Unclear methods discussion	Discuss the participants and how they were recruited. Clarify dependent, independent, and control variables. Show how you plan to do data or statistical analyses, or visualizations. Show how you analyzed your qualitative data through coding and searching for themes.
10	Difficult-to-find resources	See where you can obtain access to archived documents. Look at the available sources first before proceeding to the research proper.

PRESENTATION AND ANALYSIS

	Mistakes	*Remedies*
1	Fabricated or inaccurate data	Do not input your own data, write observations or interviews that did not happen, selectively submit results, or hide negative findings. Always verify information you write in your research.
2	Incorrect figures	Note the differences between doing bar graphs, histograms, pie charts, line graphs, and other data visualization techniques. Beware of figures without titles, labels, clear sources, and with no focus.
3	Incorrect tables	Distinguish tables for descriptive statistics, frequency, correlations, and regressions. Clarify the dependent variable. Write the statistical significance (e.g. *** $p < 0.001$). Order and group similar variables.
4	Absent or unrelated data explanation	Describe which part of the tables the reader should focus on. Organize your results section according to the progression of the tables. Write about sample size, means and standard deviations, percentages, trends, coefficients, and p-values. Be careful with using causal language.
5	Incorrect use of quotes	Beware of having too many or too few quotes. Clarify whether you are using a block quote or a regular quote. Talk about themes and supplement them with quotes or narratives. You may paraphrase or summarize long quotes.
6	Non-identified informants	For qualitative research, identify your research participant or informant. Provide information about background characteristics that may affect their answers. Some participants may be identified by name because of their expertise or position.

7	Plagiarism	Beware of the different types of plagiarism. If it is a verbatim quote, put it in quotation marks. Cite the sources of your ideas or information. Paraphrase accurately and in your own words.
8	Absent or unclear discussion section	Remind the reader about the question and argument. Synthesize findings and deeper meanings. Connect results to broader insights. Note unexpected findings and alternative explanations.
9	Inability to engage counterarguments	Provide a space to share opposing opinions. You can refute these counterarguments in your research. Be careful with having too many twists and turns in your research.
10	Research question remains unanswered	Go back to your research question and reflect on whether you were able to answer it, or whether the research was consistent with your original question.

WRITING

	Mistakes	Remedies
1	Informal tone and language	Be consistent with the use of first-person or third-person pronouns. If you use pronouns, do so sparingly. Avoid words that are obligating, direct, inaccurate, or exaggerated.
2	Unclear point	Use the point index to clarify your thesis statement. Try to underline the main point for every paragraph and see if there is coherence among paragraphs. Use the point index in structuring your ideas.
3	Unconnected paragraphs and sentences	Use transition expressions (like accordingly, despite this, although, as a matter of fact...). Be conscious of how your old information interacts with your new information. Outline broad ideas and show how the next sentences or paragraphs are connected.
4	Mistakes with sentence construction	Keep the subject and verb close to each other. Know which common tenses are used for research. Always check whether the sentences express a complete thought. Identify the modifier, and see if the word closest is the word it truly modifies. Vary the length and structure of your sentences.
5	Mistakes with words	Avoid contractions, abbreviations, and acronyms (that have not been defined). Go for concise writing rather than wordy writing. Be careful with interchangeable and technical words.

6	Mistakes with italics, bold, and underline	Use italics for light emphasis and bold for heavy emphasis. Use italics for book titles, journal titles, cinematic productions, television programs, and art work. In addition, use italics also for foreign words, scientific names, and some statistical notations.
7	Mistakes in punctuation	Semicolons are used to join two complete ideas. Colons are used to introduce a list, show emphasis, or introduce a quote. Hyphens are used to connect two or more words. Dashes are used to create a break in the structure of the sentence. Parentheses are for added clarification. Quotation marks are used for repeating a quote verbatim or short articles. Apostrophes are used to show possession.
8	Mistakes in footnote citations	Check whether you have all the correct details. Refer to the formatting guide. Use a citation management system.
9	Mistakes with in-text citation	Be familiar with the conventions of using parenthetical citations. Ensure that you have all cited sources in your bibliography.

PUBLICATION

	Mistakes	*Remedies*
1	Submitting to the wrong journal	Assess the fit between your research and the journal's aims. Review the journal's impact factor, review speed, acceptance rate, instructions, and readership. Assess whether your research is publication-ready.
2	Submitting to two journals at the same time	Do not submit to more than one journal at a time.
3	Absent or unclear abstracts	Ensure that your abstract talks about the research's purpose, design/methodology, findings, implications, and originality.
4	Weak cover letter	Write a professional letter about why the research fits the journal you are submitting to.
5	Undisclosed conflicts of interest	Disclose possible conflicts of interest that could have arisen from any monetary exchange or benefit from doing the research.
6	Disregarding reviewer comments	Familiarize yourself with the possible decisions for your submitted manuscript. When asked to revise, highlight the revisions made and show what have changed in your research.
7	Resting on your laurels	Continue to research and be productive in your scholarship.

ENDNOTES

1 Ted O'Donoghue and Matthew Rabin, "The Economics of Immediate Gratification," *Journal of Behavioral Decision Making* 13, no. 2 (April 1, 2000): 233–50, https://doi.org/10.1002/(SICI)1099-0771(200004/06)13:2<233::AID-BDM325>3.0.CO;2-U.

2 Thomas M. Brinthaupt and Chul M. Shin, "The Relationship of Academic Cramming to Flow Experience," *College Student Journal* 35, no. 3 (September 2001), https://link.galegroup.com/apps/doc/A80744659/AONE?u=googlescholar&sid=AONE&xid=744faece; Adam Grant, *Originals: How Non-Conformists Move the World* (New York: Penguin, 2016).

3 Dominic Voge, "Classroom Resources for Addressing Procrastination," *Research and Teaching in Developmental Education* 23, no. 2 (2007): 91.

4 See: Wendelien van Eerde et al., "A Review of the Time Management Literature," *Personnel Review* 36, no. 2 (February 13, 2007): 255–76, https://doi.org/10.1108/00483480710726136; Harvard Business Review, *Time Management: Increase Your Personal Productivity And Effectiveness* (Cambridge, MA: Harvard Business Press, 2005); Alec Mackenzie and Pat Nickerson, *The Time Trap: The Classic Book on Time Management* (New York: AMACOM, 2009).

5 Dominic Voge, "Changing Self-Talk in Order to Overcome Procrastination," *Research and Teaching in Developmental Education* 26, no. 2 (2010): 50–54.

6 Justin B. Dimick, "Leading Teams Effectively: Motivating and Prioritizing Work," in *Leadership in Surgery*, ed. Melina R. Kibbe and Herbert Chen, Success in Academic Surgery (Cham: Springer International Publishing, 2015), 99–106, https://doi.org/10.1007/978-3-319-11107-0_9.

7 Edwin R. van Teijlingen and Vanora Hundley, "The Importance of Pilot Studies," *Social Research Update* 35 (2001), http://aura.abdn.ac.uk/handle/2164/157.

8 Siri Vinther and Jacob Rosenberg, "Appearance of Ghost and Gift Authors in Ugeskrift for Læger and Danish Medical Journal," *Danish Medical Journal* 59, no. 5 (2012): 1.

9 Martin McKneally, "Put My Name on That Paper: Reflections on the Ethics of Authorship," *The Journal of Thoracic and Cardiovascular Surgery* 131, no. 3 (March 1, 2006): 517, https://doi.org/10.1016/j.jtcvs.2005.09.060.

10 Dianne M. Bennett and David McD Taylor, "Unethical Practices in Authorship of Scientific Papers," *Emergency Medicine* 15, no. 3 (June 1, 2003): 263–70, https://doi.org/10.1046/j.1442-2026.2003.00432.x.

11 Emile Durkheim, *Suicide: A Study in Sociology* (New York: Routledge, 2005).

12 Anna S. Mueller, Seth Abrutyn, and Cynthia Stockton, "Can Social Ties Be Harmful? Examining the Spread of Suicide in Early Adulthood," *Sociological Perspectives* 58, no. 2 (June 1, 2015): 204–22, https://doi.org/10.1177/0731121414556544.

13 Harriet Churchill and Teela Sanders, *Getting Your PhD: A Practical Insider's Guide* (New York: SAGE, 2007), 29.

14 Richard J. Lilford and Jennifer Jackson, "Equipoise and the Ethics of Randomization," *Journal of the Royal Society of Medicine* 88, no. 10 (October 1995): 552.

15 Lou Antolihao, *Playing with the Big Boys: Basketball, American Imperialism, and Subaltern Discourse in the Philippines* (Quezon City: Ateneo de Manila University Press, 2017).

16 J.A. Khan, *Research Methodology* (New Delhi: APH Publishing, 2011).

17 Michael K. Le Roy, *Research Methods in Political Science: An Introduction Using MicroCase* (Boston, MA: Thomson Wadsworth, 2008).

18 Kevin Durrheim, "Research Design," in *Research in Practice: Applied Methods for the Social Sciences*, ed. Martin Terre Blanche, Kevin Durrheim and Desmond Painter (Cape Town: University of Cape Town Press, 2006), 36.

19 This is a fictional character but this was inspired by the written work of some students.

20 Gabriela Saldanha and Sharon O'Brien, *Research Methodologies in Translation Studies* (London and New York: Routledge, 2013).

21 Jane Hsieh and Jason K. Lee, "Chronic Spontaneous Urticaria," *Canadian Medical Association Journal* 189, no. 2 (January 16, 2017): E77–E77, https://doi.org/10.1503/cmaj.150951.

22 Jose Eos Trinidad, "Structural Limitations and Functional Alternatives Reducing Suspensions and Preserving Racial Suspension Gaps," *Race Ethnicity and Education* online first (October 24, 2018): 1–16, https://doi.org/10.1080/13613324.2018.1538119.

23 Robert Faux, "Quantitative Research," in *Encyclopedia of Critical Psychology*, ed. Thomas Teo (New York, NY: Springer New York, 2014), 1615, http://link.springer.com/10.1007/978-1-4614-5583-7.

24 Chris Hart, *Doing a Literature Review: Releasing the Social Science Research Imagination* (London: SAGE, 1998), 13, http://www.tandfonline.com/doi/abs/10.1080/09500790.2011.588012.

25 Inspired by: Elizabeth F. Barkley and Claire H. Major, *Interactive Lecturing: A Handbook for College Faculty* (San Francisco, CA: John Wiley & Sons, 2018).

26 Jose L. Galvan, *Writing Literature Reviews: A Guide for Students of the Social and Behavioral Sciences* (London and New York: Routledge, 2016)."

27 Sheila Cameron and Deborah Price, *Business Research Methods: A Practical Approach* (London: Chartered Institute of Personnel and Development, 2009).

28 It has to be clarified, however, that this peer-review process is not always foolproof. There are some research that actually get published but have inaccurate or deceptive findings. Nonetheless, this process has been relied upon and has generally been quite helpful for knowledge-production.

29 Joseph Maxwell, "Foreword," in Sharon Ravitch and Matthew Riggan, *Reason and Rigor: How Conceptual Frameworks Guide Research* (Los Angeles: SAGE, 2016).

30 Tonette S. Rocco and Maria Plakhotnik, "Literature Reviews, Conceptual Frameworks, and Theoretical Frameworks: Terms, Functions, and Distinctions," *Human Resource Development Review* (March 2009): 120-130.

31 Howard S. Becker, *Tricks of the Trade: How to think about your research while you're doing it.* (Chicago, IL: University of Chicago Press, 1998).

32 For a more thorough discussion of these, you can refer to the section on data analysis or on the companion book to this present book: Jose Eos Trinidad, *Researching Philippine Realities: A Guide to Qualitative, Quantitative, and Humanities Research* (Quezon City: Bluebooks/ Ateneo de Manila University Press, 2018).

33 Janice D. Aurini, Melanie Heath, and Stephanie Howells, *The How To of Qualitative Research* (London: SAGE, 2016).

34 John W. Creswell and J. David Creswell, *Research Design: Qualitative, Quantitative, and Mixed Methods Approaches, 5th edition* (London: SAGE, 2017).

35 W. Paul Vogt, Dianne C. Gardner and Lynne M, Haeffele, *When to Use What Research Design* (New York, NY: Guilford Press, 2012).

36 Sharon L. Lohr, *Sampling: Design and Analysis, 2nd Edition* (Boston: Brookes/Cole, 2010).

37 Stephen D. Lapan, Marlynn T. Quartaroli, and Frances J. Riemer, ed. *Qualitative Research: An Introduction to Methods and Design* (San Francisco, CA: John Wiley and Sons, 2012).

38 Raji Swaminathan and Thalia M. Mulvihill, *Critical Approaches to Questions in Qualitative Research* (New York, NY: Routledge, 2017).

39 Gary T. Henry, *Practical Sampling – Applied Social Research Methods Series Volume 21* (Newbury Park, CA: SAGE, 1990).

40 David S. Festinger and David DeMatteo, "Subject Selection," in *Evidence-Based Outcome Research: A Practical Guide to Conducting Randomized Controlled Trials for Psychosocial Interventions* (Oxford: Oxford University Press, 2008).

41 Mark L. Mitchell and Janina M. Jolley, *Research Design Explained, 7th Edition* (Belmont, CA: Wadsworth, 2010).

42 Monique M. Hennink, *Understanding Focus Group Discussions* (Oxford: Oxford University Press, 2014).

43 Chauncey Wilson, *Interview Techniques for UX Practitioners: A User-Centered Design Method* (Waltham, MA: Morgan Kaufmann, 2014).

44 Johnny Saldana, *The Coding Manual for Qualitative Researchers* (Thousand Oaks, CA: SAGE, 2015).

45 D.J. Harris and G. Atkinson, "Ethical Standards in Sport and Exercise Science Research: 2016 Update," *International Journal of Sports Medicine* 36, no. 14 (2015): 1121–24.

46 Robert L. Berger, "Nazi Science — The Dachau Hypothermia Experiments," *New England Journal of Medicine* 322, no. 20 (May 17, 1990): 1435–40, https://doi.org/10.1056/NEJM199005173222006.

47 Malcolm Carey, *Qualitative Research Skills for Social Work: Theory and Practice* (New York: Routledge, 2017).

48 Deborah Zion, Lynn Gillam, and Bebe Loff, "The Declaration of Helsinki, CIOMS and the Ethics of Research on Vulnerable Populations," *Nature Medicine* 6 (June 1, 2000): 615–17, https://doi.org/10.1038/76174.

49 Mary Ann Boyd, *Psychiatric Nursing: Contemporary Practice* (Philadelphia, PA: Lippincott Williams & Wilkins, 2005).

50 Anne Harrington, "Introduction," in *The Placebo Effect: An Interdisciplinary Exploration*, ed. Anne Harrington (Cambridge, MA: Harvard University Press, 1999).

51 Chava Frankfort-Nachmias and Anna Leon-Guerrero, *Social Statistics for a Diverse Society, 8th Edition* (Thousand Oaks, CA: SAGE, 2018).

52 Katherine Michelmore and Susan Dynarski, "The Gap within the Gap: Using Longitudinal Data to Understand Income Differences in Student Achievement," 2016; Dana Wood, Rachel Kaplan, and Vonnie C. McLoyd, "Gender Differences in the Educational Expectations of Urban, Low-Income African American Youth: The Role of Parents and the School," *Journal of Youth and Adolescence* 36, no. 4 (May 1, 2007): 417–27, https://doi.org/10.1007/s10964-007-9186-2; J. Estudillo, A. Quisumbing, and K. Otsuka, "Gender Differences in Land Inheritance, Schooling and Lifetime Income: Evidence from the Rural Philippines," *The Journal of Development Studies* 37, no. 4 (April 1, 2001): 23–48, https://doi.org/10.1080/00220380412331322031; Futoshi Yamauchi and Marites Tiongco, "Why Women Are Progressive in Education? Gender Disparities in Human Capital, Labor Markets, and Family Arrangement in the Philippines," *Economics of Education Review* 32 (February 1, 2013): 196–206, https://doi.org/10.1016/j.econedurev.2012.09.003.

53 Judith Greene and Manuela D'Oliveira, *Learning to Use Statistical Tests in Psychology* (Berkshire, England: Open University Press, 2005).

54 David de Vaus, *Analyzing Social Science Data: 50 Key Problems in Data Analysis* (London: SAGE, 2002).

55 Deborah J. Rumsey, "What a P-Value Tells You about Statistical Data," *Dummies* (blog), accessed December 20, 2018, https://www.dummies.com/education/math/statistics/what-a-p-value-tells-you-about-statistical-data/.

56 Robert H. Brookshire and Shelley B. Brundage, *Writing Scientific Research in Communication Sciences and Disorder* (San Diego, CA: Plural Publishing, 2015).

57 National Academies of Sciences, Engineering, and Medicine et al., *Fostering Integrity in Research* (Washington, DC: National Academies Press, 2018).

58 Victoria E. McMillan, *Writing Papers in the Biological Sciences* (New York: St. Martin's, 2016).

59 Daniel Powers and Yu Xie, *Statistical Methods for Categorical Data Analysis* (Bingley, UK: Emerald Group Publishing, 2008).

60 Lab Write Resources, "Graphing -Designing Tables," North Carolina State University, 2004, https://projects.ncsu.edu/labwrite/res/gh/gh-tables.html.

61 Earl Babbie, *The Basics of Social Research* (Belmont, CA: Thomson Higher Education, 2008).

62 Robert V. Labaree, "Research Guides: Organizing Your Social Sciences Research Paper: 7. The Results," Research Guide, University of Southern California Libraries, 2018, //libguides.usc.edu/writingguide/results; David R. Caprette, "Common Errors Found in Student Research Papers," Rice University, 2005, https://www.ruf.rice.edu/~bioslabs/tools/report/reporterror.html.

63 American Psychological Association, *Publication Manual of the American Psychological Association* (Washington, DC: American Psychological Association, 2006).

64 Jesper Aagaard, "Drawn to Distraction: A Qualitative Study of Off-Task Use of Educational Technology," *Computers & Education* 87 (September 1, 2015): 90–97, https://doi.org/10.1016/j.compedu.2015.03.010.

65 Wendy Sutherland-Smith, *Plagiarism, the Internet, and Student Learning: Improving Academic Integrity* (London: Routledge, 2008).

66 John Walker, "Student Plagiarism in Universities: What Are We Doing About It?," *Higher Education Research & Development* 17, no. 1 (April 1, 1998): 89–106, https://doi.org/10.1080/0729436980170105.

67 "What Is Plagiarism?," Plagiarism.org, May 18, 2017, http://www.plagiarism.org/article/what-is-plagiarism.

68 Robert Putnam, *Bowling Alone: The Collapse and Revival of American Community* (New York: Simon and Schuster, 2000).

69 Ken K. Wong, *Avoiding Plagiarism: Write Better Papers in Apa, Chicago, and Harvard Citation Styles* (Bloomington, IN: iUniverse, 2011).

70 John Bitchener and Helen Basturkmen, "Perceptions of the Difficulties of Postgraduate L2 Thesis Students Writing the Discussion Section," *Journal of English for Academic Purposes* 5 (January 2006): 4–18; Thomas M. Annesley, "The Discussion Section: Your Closing Argument," *Clinical Chemistry* 56, no. 7 (November 2010): 1671–74.

71 Robert J. MacCoun, "Biases in the Interpretation and Use of Research Results," *Annual Review of Psychology* 49, no. 1 (February 1998): 259–87.

72 American Psychological Association, *Publication Manual of the American Psychological Association.*

73 Manik Joshi, *Transitional Words and Phrases: Using Transitional Expressions* (India: Manik Joshi, 2016).

74 Jennifer Peat et al., *Scientific Writing: Easy When You Know How* (San Francisco, CA: John Wiley & Sons, 2013).

75 Paige Wilson and Teresa Glazier, *The Least You Should Know about English: Writing Skills, Form A* (Cengage Learning, 2008).

76 Adrian Wallwork, *English for Writing Research Papers*, 2nd edition (Heidelberg: Springer, 2016).

77 Margaret Cargill and Patrick O'Connor, *Writing Scientific Research Articles: Strategy and Steps* (San Francisco, CA: John Wiley & Sons, 2009).

78 John M. Swales and Christine B. Feak, *Academic Writing for Graduate Students: Essential Tasks and Skills* (Ann Arbor: University of Michigan Press, 2012).

79 "Informal Language | Oxford Dictionaries," Oxford Dictionaries | English, accessed December 28, 2018, https://en.oxforddictionaries.com/usage/informal-language.

80 From Nicholas Pak, Writing a Great Paper and Getting it Published (a workshop sponsored by Elsevier at Ateneo de Manila University last November 28, 2018).

81 Wilson and Glazier, *The Least You Should Know about English.*

82 Kristina Pfleegor, "Research Guides: Grammar, Punctuation, and Sentences: Beyond Commas (Other Punctuation Marks)," July 30, 2018, https://research.ewu.edu/c.php?g=425370&p=2905515.

83 University of Chicago Press Editorial Staff, *The Chicago Manual of Style* (Chicago: University of Chicago Press, 2017); Jose Eos Trinidad, *Researching Philippine Realities: A Guide to Qualitative, Quantitative, and Humanities Research* (Quezon City: Bluebooks, 2018).

84 Michael John, "The Target Journal: Choosing the Right Place to Submit Your Paper," *HSR Proceedings in Intensive Care & Cardiovascular Anesthesia* 1, no. 3 (2009): 60–62.

85 Elizabeth Wager, "Why You Should Not Submit Your Work to More than One Journal at a Time," *African Journal of Traditional, Complementary, and Alternative Medicines* 7, no. 2 (December 30, 2009): 160–61.

86 SAGE, "9 Publishing Basics for Anyone Submitting to a Scholarly Journal," SAGE Connection – Insight (blog), November 5, 2013, https://connection.sagepub.com/blog/sage-connection/2013/11/05/9-publishing-basics-for-anyone-submitting-to-a-scholarly-journal/.

87 Michael John, "I Really Think You Should Publish This Paper: The Cover Letter to the Editor," *HSR Proceedings in Intensive Care & Cardiovascular Anesthesia* 3, no. 2 (2011): 137–39.

88 Paul L. Romain, "Conflicts of Interest in Research: Looking out for Number One Means Keeping the Primary Interest Front and Center," *Current Reviews in Musculoskeletal Medicine* 8, no. 2 (April 8, 2015): 122–27, https://doi.org/10.1007/s12178-015-9270-2.

89 Brian Paltridge, *The Discourse of Peer Review: Reviewing Submissions to Academic Journals* (London: Palgrave Macmillan, 2017).

INDEX

ACKNOWLEDGMENTS

Even if most outsiders think that research and intellectual investigation is a very solitary endeavor—and sometimes, it can really be like that—I have been privileged to receive the support of many friends who have, in one way or another, been sources of support, encouragement, mentorship, and generosity of thought. This present book is itself the product of these friendships and mutual support.

I extend my thanks to various professors in the Ateneo de Manila University whose insights into researchers and students' mistakes have formed the backbone of the book: Didith Rodrigo of the Department of Information Systems and Computer Science; Mark Joseph Calano of the Department of Philosophy; Kristin Militante of the Department of Finance and Accounting; Rhoda Nicdao of the Department of Education; Emma Porio of the Department of Sociology and Anthropology; Arvin Boller of the Department of Psychology; and Cecile Ilagan of the Ateneo Journals' Office. Thank you very much for generously sharing and commenting on the outline of this book.

Other colleagues from the Ateneo de Manila have also shown great enthusiasm with this project, particularly my colleagues at the Department of Interdisciplinary Studies (Rofel Brion, Marichi Guevara, Nikki Carsi Cruz, Jonathan Chua, and Soledad Reyes) and the Institute for the Science and Art of Learning and Teaching (Fr. Johnny Go, Rita Atienza, Galvin Ngo, Je Ching, Solvie Nubla-Lee, and Jen Ramirez). I also extend my thanks to people who have given valuable comments on the early manuscripts: Carlo Mallari of Nara Institute of Science and Technology and Joshua Uyheng of the Carnegie Mellon University.

Aside from colleagues in the academe, research teachers from all over the Philippines have also helped by sharing their comments and ideas on common research mistakes. Thanks to Kian Calvin Tunaya, Cladys Falcunaya, Arvin Diamante, Krephel Navales, Jeric Ilao, Jonathan Diokno, Johna Venus, Ghellina Cleofe, Jeremy James Sim, Lou Cristobal Cruz, Den Mark Peligro, Rhejay Macatangay, Ruby Flores, Ito Serizawa, Arnold Antiporda, Francis Domingo, Mark Alvin Cruz, and the many teachers working in private and public schools. These teachers who are in college and high school classrooms are the true heroes to whom this book is dedicated.

When you do research, many unnamed people will be there to help and support you. In the same way, I have been so blessed to be instructed by journal editors, reviewers, and proofreaders who were more than gracious in pointing out my own research mistakes. Most of these people I have not met in person nor have I had the privilege of corresponding at length. Nonetheless, their assistance is strongly felt and their insights have influenced the discussion in this book.

Despite the faceless or nameless people I interact with when doing research, I have been reminded of the humanity of the people working in the publishing industry through the process of writing this manuscript. I extend my thanks to the many people at the Ateneo de Manila University Press who have helped bring this present book to completion. Thanks to Karina Bolasco for your helpful comments on the direction of the book; to Nieves Darroca and Tina Castro for your encouragement and for keeping this manuscript on track; to Kevin Dy, Anne San Agustin, and your whole team for the fantastic work with the first book; and to Gemma Roces for all the assistance. My thanks also extend to Randy Bustamante for the helpful editorial comments, Mikaela Montano for the creative book cover, and Cielo Castro for the engaging layout.

Many other people deserve my thanks, not the least of which are Philip, Ellen, Ino, Yya, and Ely. Their patience and support are only second to none. *Dios mabalos!*